VOID

Library of
Davidson College

Series / Number 90-007

Legislative-Executive Policy-Making:
The Cases of Chile and Costa Rica

STEVEN W. HUGHES
California State College, Stanlislaus

KENNETH J. MIJESKI
East Tennessee State University

SAGE PUBLICATIONS / Beverly Hills / London

Copyright © 1973 by Sage Publications, Inc.

Printed in the United States of America

All rights reserved. No part of this book may be reproduced or utilized in any form or by any means, electronic or mechanical, including photocopying, recording, or by any information storage and retrieval system, without permission in writing from the publisher.

For information address:

SAGE PUBLICATIONS, INC.
275 South Beverly Drive
Beverly Hills, California 90212

SAGE PUBLICATIONS, INC.
St George's House / 44 Hatton Garden
London EC1N 8ER

International Standard Book Number 0-8039-0365-0

Library of Congress Catalog No. L.C. 73-92221

FIRST PRINTING

When citing a professional paper, please use the proper form. Remember to cite the correct Sage Professional Paper series title and include the paper number. One of the two following formats can be adapted (depending on the style manual used):

(1) KORNBERG, A. et al. (1973) "Legislatures and Societal Change: The Case of Canada." Sage Research Papers in the Social Sciences (Comparative Legislative Studies Series, No. 90-002). Beverly Hills and London: Sage Pubns.

OR

(2) Kornberg, Allan et al. 1973. *Legislatures and Societal Change: The Case of Canada.* Sage Research Papers in the Social Sciences, vol. 1, series no. 90-002 (Comparative Legislative Studies Series). Beverly Hills and London: Sage Publications.

Contents

Introduction *5*

Relative Dominance: A Conceptual Framework *7*

Chile *11*

    Policy Initiation *11*
    Policy Modification *13*
    Policy Acceptance or Rejection *16*
    Policy Review *17*
    Policy as Executive Decrees *18*
    An Overview and an Attempt at Explanation *20*

Costa Rica *27*

    Methods and Procedures *27*
    Policy Initiation *28*
    Policy Modification *32*
    Policy Acceptance or Rejection *36*
    Policy Review *37*
    Policy as Executive Decrees *38*
    An Overview and an Attempt at Explanation *40*

Comparing Relative Dominance in Chile and Costa Rica: Summary and Conclusions *48*

    Accounting for Differences *49*
    Suggestions for Further Research *53*

Notes *54*

References *56*

LEGISLATIVE-EXECUTIVE POLICY-MAKING
The Cases of Chile and Costa Rica

STEVEN W. HUGHES

California State College, Stanlislaus

KENNETH J. MIJESKI

East Tennessee State University

Introduction

This study is an attempt to assess the roles of the executive and legislative branches in policy-making in Chile and Costa Rica between 1958 and 1970. The basic rationale for this study is twofold. In the first place, the rationale lies in the authors' interests in understanding policy-making and the groups involved in the process. Policy-making and policy decisions are generally conceded to be a primary concern of political scientists (Bauer and Gergen, 1968). In fact, if we take the political systems framework as establishing the main outlines of political research, it becomes quite apparent that policy is at the center of our interests. To understand this process, it is necessary to know who the actors are and what roles they play, especially if the actors are reputed to be important in the policy process (Ranney, 1968).

A focus on the legislature and executive has been chosen not only because they are supposed to be important in formulating policy, but also because they are the most visible and among the most accessible. And the advantages of accessibility are many, particularly regarding the trials and tribulations of data collection. In effect, we are simply arguing that an analysis of the relative decisional positions of the congress and of the executive is crucial to an understanding of policy-making in Chile and Costa Rica.

AUTHORS' NOTE: This study is actually an attempt to integrate two previously separate studies (Hughes, 1971; Mijeski, 1971). Originally, the authors tried to make their studies parallel; however, situational factors forced approaches not entirely identical. In terms of specific measurement, variables, and data, the studies do diverge somewhat; hence, the findings for each country are reported separately. The section entitled "Relative Dominance: A Conceptual Framework" concentrates on those concepts commonly employed. Concepts used in one study but not in the other are discussed in the section about the country to which they were applied.

While the primary motivating force for this study lies in an interest in decision-making, a second inducement lies in the paucity of adequate empirical knowledge of decision-making in Latin America. In particular, such knowledge is scant regarding the decisional relationship of the executive and legislative branches. Until quite recently, conventional wisdom has all but assigned Latin-American legislatures to policy-making oblivion. Studies by Rosendo Gómez (1961), Robert Scott (1958), Alexander Edelmann (1969), and others have consistently emphasized the executive's policy-making dominance. It is true that some other studies, such as Gil's (1966), Tomasek's (1968) and Busey's (1962), have specifically exempted both the Costa Rican and Chilean legislatures from policy obscurity; nevertheless, these works are neither detailed nor systematic in their analyses of the executive-legislative relationship.

Within the last three years, our awareness of the potential import of certain Latin-American legislatures—particularly those of Costa Rica and Chile—has been substantially increased through the volumes edited by Kornberg and Musolf (1970), Agor (1971a), and Kornberg (1973). Of these three, the Agor volume is probably the most interesting because it concentrates entirely on Latin-American legislatures. Furthermore, the various studies are focused on an attempt to explicate the legislature's decisional role. Given the previous paucity of such information, this effort certainly deserves to be labeled an important breakthrough. Yet, as the excellent review by Ann Schultz (1972) pointedly notes, only the article on Costa Rica by Christopher Baker approaches an empirical documentation of the decisional role. And Baker (1971: 15) himself comments on the exploratory nature of his research.

In no way do we wish to belittle the research undertaken recently on the congresses of Latin America.[1] Nor, certainly, do we desire to suggest that our study offers the definitive solution. We do suggest, however, that much remains to be done, especially with regard to those legislatures tentatively established as important policy-makers. As Patterson and Wahlke (1972: 291) recently stated, "Gaps in knowledge about legislative institutions and behavior are enormous." These gaps of knowledge exist in both the area of basic description and the area of explanation. Lowenberg (1972: 16), for instance, notes that while such variables as party organization have been related to legislative behavor, "a brief review of research on these variables does, however, suggest the fragmentary manner in which these variables are generally linked to the pattern of legislative behavior they are presumably designed to explain." In addition, Patterson and Wahlke rightly point out a great need for more conceptual work and the problems involved in "mapping comparative legislative research strategy."

Convinced that the valuable work undertaken by Agor (1971)[2] and Baker (1971) has demonstrated both the need and the potential payoff of further research on the Chilean and Costa Rican legislatures, this study attempts to further investigate the issue. Convinced too that our knowledge will be particularly advanced by a systematic conceptual approach, this study emphasizes a conceptually-oriented description of relative decisional dominance in Costa Rica and Chile. More specifically, this essay attempts to (1) clarify the concept of relative dominance in policy-making, (2) propose a conceptual framework within which the question of relative dominance might be more usefully examined, (3) seek an answer to the question, is either the executive or the legislature dominant in the institutional policy-making process in Chile and Costa Rica?, (4) suggest the possible relationship between certain institutional and contextual variables and the phenomenon of relative dominance. The emphasis, however, is on the first three goals.

RELATIVE DOMINANCE: A CONCEPTUAL FRAMEWORK

A general decline in the decisional position of the legislature has been observed by many students of legislative behavior. In a vein similar to the studies on Latin America, Western European observers have suggested that these legislatures also exert little leverage in the formulation of public policy. Lindberg (1966: 101-128) argues that these parliaments "neither make laws nor exercise effective control over the executive." Carl Friedrich (1950: 3), while noting the once powerful position held by parliaments at an earlier time, observes that the executive is now moving ahead and taking over center stage in the governmental process. And as Samuel Beer (1966: 33) succinctly says, "In Britain this is an age not of parliamentary government, but of cabinet government."

According to some, the United States Congress has also lost power. One analyst (Robinson, 1962: 8) has remarked that "Congress' role . . . [is] less and less one of the initiation of policy and more and more the modifier, negator, or legitimator of proposals which originate in the executive."

There are others, however, who have argued that the United States Congress has not witnessed any decline in its decisional position. Griffith (1967), for example, states that the growth of various congressional staffs and service agencies has given to Congress the expertise needed to maintain its role vis-a-vis the executive. Huitt (1966) also supports this contention while speaking of the Congress as the "durable partner."

As this discussion suggests, there are different ways of viewing the question of relative decisional dominance. Moreover, it seems apparent that the differing conclusions may arise precisely because the nature of the executive-legislative relationship varies depending upon which phase or aspect of the policy process one is talking about. Accepting this conclusion, it is useful to construct an explicit "policy stage" variable within which the dependent variable, relative decisional dominance, might be more systematically appraised. The following formulation is proposed for the present study: (1) initiation, (2) modification, (3) acceptance-rejection, (4) review. For the present, we shall limit our discussion to the law-making dimension of the policy process.

The initiation stage is simply that stage in which a policy proposal officially originates. In both Chile and Costa Rica, bills are marked to indicate whether they were presented by a legislator or a member of the executive branch. Relative dominance is measured in this stage by comparing the percentage of bills initiated by the executive with those initiated by the legislature. This measurement, of course, ignores the more subtle ramifications of the initiation dimension, such as where the idea or initial draft actually originated. Unfortunately, to unravel the claims and counterclaims for originality would take an entire treatise itself.

The second stage of the policy process involves the area of modification. This stage centers around legislative committee-executive interaction as well as party leaders-executive interchanges. Within the legislature, discussions among party leaders, committee chairmen, and other legislative officers may well take place. This is the bargaining stage of the policy process, probably centering in the actions of legislative committees[3] but including bargaining on the floor of the legislature. In this stage of policy-making, executive-legislative relations become entangled with intralegislative interactions. Unlike the initiation stage where relative dominance of one over the other is a simple either-or proposition, the modification stage may open up more points of access for attempts at executive persuasion, depending on the internal distribution of influence within the legislative body. Nevertheless, we can still conceive of the process in terms of the executive vis-a-vis the legislature.

In assessing relative dominance on this dimension, we utilize two types of measurement. At the most obvious level, an attempt is made to simply assess the number of executive and legislative proposals which have been modified or altered. In addition, we seek to make a qualitative assessment by analyzing the occurrence of significant modifications. By significant, we refer to those modifications that alter the original nature or purpose of the bill or so alter a relatively important substantive or procedural section of the bill.

The next stage, acceptance-rejection, is largely self-explanatory. Bargaining is completed; modifications have been proposed and either accepted or rejected. All that remains is a simple yes-no choice on the part of the whole legislature. The measure of relative dominance at this stage is simply a comparison of two ratios: the ratio of defeated to total executive bills compared to the same ratio for those bills initiated by the legislature.[4]

Review is the final stage of the policy process. It occurs after a bill has left the legislative arena of bill-making as outlined above, and has become an operating law administered by the executive branch or, in Chile and Costa Rica, by autonomous or semi-autonomous agencies. At this stage, the legislature may become reinvolved if a particular agency's interpretation of "policy" is at odds with what was "intended" by the legislature. The interactions that take place in this stage are likely to be of the legislative committee-executive agency variety.

This particular dimension of the policy process has been a focal point for much research in the United States (see, Inter alia, Freeman, 1966; Bibby, 1966; Scher, 1963). Sharkansky (1965), for example, proposes a simple though somewhat roundabout measure of this dimension. Unfortunately, this analysis would have required more research time than was available. Furthermore, few data exist in Chile and Costa Rica to systematically measure this dimension. Consequently, only scanty and, by and large, impressionistic evidence will be offered, primarily from several interviews with Chilean and Costa Rican legislators.

At this point we shall expand our concept of policy to include a widely used device in Chile and, to a somewhat lesser extent, in Costa Rica: the executive decree. In a sense, executive decree are simply executive policy-making. That is, while both the executive and legislature take part in the law-making process, the executive can often circumvent that process by issuing decrees that have the force of law but do not require the participation of the legislative branch. Decrees, then, may be conceptualized as purely executive decisions and laws as legislative decisions, though not purely legislative. Because laws are not purely legislative, viewing them as such will tend to "underestimate" executive leverage. We have already discussed this in the section outlining measures of relative dominance in each stage of the policy-making (law-making) process. With the addition of decrees, we can suggest a general quantity of output measure by comparing the total number of executive decrees and resolutions with the total number of laws.[5] We hope doing so will give us a broader dimension of relative dominance that, if omitted from consideration, would ignore an important part of the executive's leverage over policy-making.[6]

Within the context of our effort to measure relative policy dominance, we have also sought to make qualitative distinctions regarding output. While one institution might produce a much greater quantity of output, its decisional position would not be stronger if its output were qualitatively inferior. Our criteria for the qualitative distinctions were borrowed from Polsby (1963: 95-96).

According to Polsby, decisions can be ranked in importance by "making use of one or another, or a combination, of at least four criteria: (1) how many people are affected by the outcomes; (2) how many different kinds of community resources are distributed by outcomes; (3) how much in amount of resources are distributed by outcomes; (4) how drastically present community resource distributions are altered by outcomes."

In the final analysis, the scheme has been utilized on a basically intuitive and commonsense basis. It is very difficult to provide objective and satisfactory cutoff points for each criterion. Rather, we find that while some decisions are obviously unimportant and others important, still other decisions lie in a very ambiguous "middle-range."

In summary, we have sought to establish a framework by which to analyze, conceptualize, and measure relative dominance. The essence of the framework consists of two parts. First, construct a policy stage variable to measure dominance in terms of policy (i.e., law) initiation, modification, acceptance-rejection, and review. Second, analyze policy dominance in terms of the total quantity of output (including comparing output of laws with executive decrees).

As mentioned previously, the focus of the study is on describing and understanding the nature of policy dominance. In the next two sections, the data presented are, primarily, for the purpose of measuring relative dominance. However, it is also important to know why one or the other institution is more dominant. To this end, an attempt is made to relate a number of independent variables to our dependent variable.

In a brief article on the British Parliament, Samuel Beer (1966) suggests a causal relationship between two variables and increases in the relative decisional position of the executive vis-a-vis the legislature. These variables are increases in the levels of state intervention in the economy and the growing technicality of policy decisions. Beer argues that increased levels of state intervention lead to an increase of policy decisions that are specific, complex, and technical—what he calls managerial decisions—and a concomitant decrease of general guideline-type policies. This in turn leads to a lessening of Congress' decisional role because it is better equipped to handle the nonmanagerial decisions. Thus Beer relates an independent variable (state intervention) to an intervening variable (managerial policies) and this to a dependent variable (increase in executive policy dominance). (Specific operationalizations of the independent variables are discussed below.)

In addition to the factors of state intervention and managerial policies, a number of other variables have been utilized in an attempt to explain relative dominance. Essentially, these variables have to do with size of party opposition in the legislature and the nature of the congressional systems. These variables will be discussed in greater detail in the two sections that present data for Chile and Costa Rica.

In the following sections we present our findings concerning the relative decisional positions of the executive and the legislature. The data attempt both to describe the nature of relative dominance and to explain variations in the dominance position, first in Chile, then in Costa Rica. In both instances, the principal data sources are official congressional records and interviews. Occasionally, secondary sources have also been utilized. For each country, the data are organized according to the framework established above: a description of dominance for each policy stage (initiation, modification, acceptance-rejection, and review); a description of dominance in terms of total output; an explanation of policy dominance.

CHILE

POLICY INITIATION

The vast majority of students of Chilean executive-legislative relations have come to the conclusion that the executive is quite dominant in terms of initiation. One writer (Bulnes, 1967: 131-141), for instance, notes that, whereas the Congress has numerous constitutional facilities with which it could restrain the executive's decisional role, in fact it has not done so and consequently the presidency has attained unrivaled superiority. Another student of Chilean legislative activities (Tapia, 1960: 38) also argues that Congress' initiatory role is extremely limited and that virtually all general, important laws are initiated by the executive. On the other hand, there are those who argue that the initiating role of the Congress is not so severely restricted. In a study of the Chilean Senate, Agor (1969: 236) concludes that it definitely plays a role in the initiation of legislation "despite the 1943 constitutional reform of Article 45, section 3 that supposedly gave the president exclusive initiative in public expenditures." Obviously then, there is some dispute concerning the precise initiative role played by the executive and legislature. Examining the following data might provide a more precise conclusion as to the relative dominance positions on this dimension.

In the time period studied here (1958-1970, the administration of Jorge Allesandri and Eduardo Frei), the legislature was in session all year. The year-long meetings were divided into two types of sessions (legislatures), ordinary and extraordinary. The ordinary legislatures, according to the Constitution, were opened on May 21 and closed on September 18, For the remainder of the twelve months, Congress met in extraordinary legislatures convoked by the President. In these sessions, the Congress considered only those projects approved by the President and indicated in the convocatory.[7] This does not mean that congressmen could not introduce bills, but rather, that they were required to obtain executive approval before intitiating a project.

If we look at the data for the ordinary legislatures in Table 1, we see that the overwhelming majority of bills are introduced by legislators and not by the executive. In the four years for which data have been obtained, over 91 percent of all legislation originated in Congress. And the trend has been toward a greater initiative role by Congress: approximately 89 percent of all legislation originated in Congress during the two years of

Table 1. Bills initiated by executive and legislature, ordinary legislatures

	All Bills			Important Bills		
	Executive %	Legislature %	Total N	Executive %	Legislature %	Total N
1960	10.5	89.5	261	22.1	77.9	77
1963	11.3	88.7	275	16.4	83.6	73
1966	8.4	91.6	227	21.1	78.9	57
1967	2.5	97.5	239	11.1	88.9	54
Total	8.6	91.4	1002	18.0	82.0	261

Source: Diario de Sesiones del Senado and Cámara

Jorge Alessandri's regime and 94.5 percent during the two years of Eduardo Frei's regime. Similarly, if we look only at the important bills, the dominant role is again played by Congress, which initiated 82 percent of these bills.

On the other hand, the situation changes drastically if we look at the data for extraordinary legislatures in Table 2. Because all bills initiated in these sessions must have executive approval, we may conceive of these as executive initiated. Doing so, we find that the Congress accounts for about 56 percent of all bills but only 40 percent of the *important* bills.

We have also included in Table 2 figures on bills formally introduced by legislators. These data illustrate the kind of bargaining that takes place

Table 2. Bills initiated by executive and legislature, extraordinary legislatures[a]

	All Bills					Important Bills				
	Executive		Legislature		Total	Executive		Legislature		Total
	N	%	N	%	N	N	%	N	%	N
1963-64	(155)	61.1	(99)	39.0	254	(55)	68.8	(25)	31.2	80
1964-65	(102)	53.1	(90)	46.9	192	(41)	59.4	(28)	40.6	69
1968-69	(158)	60.5	(103)	39.5	261	(79)	68.1	(37)	31.9	116
Total	(415)	58.7	(292)	41.3	707	(175)	66.0	(90)	34.0	265

[a] All bills introduced in Extraordinary Legislatures must have executive approval and, therefore, are in effect executive bills. Numbers in this table refer to bills <u>formally</u> initiated by congressmen.

even on the initiation level. Rarely will the president accept a congressional proposal if it clashes with his program. However, proposals will be accepted even when they might not completely satisfy the executive if he needs the congressman's approval for his bills. Thus, these sets of figures illustrate that even in the extraordinary legislatures the executive cannot completely dominate the initiation process.

While Congress plays a significant initiatory role, introducing a majority of bills, its influence is reduced by the fact that it plays a minor role in submitting budgetary legislation. With the exception of municipal loans, Congress rarely introduces public expenditure bills. Furthermore, about 40 percent of all public revenues and expenditures are never viewed by Congress because, rather than being in the annual budget, they correspond to autonomous and semifiscal institutions (35 percent) and to municipalities (5 percent) (Guzman, 1964: 122-123). Hence, we find that while Congress introduces a greater quantity of bills, it is the executive branch that submits the important ones.

POLICY MODIFICATION

The Chilean Congress also plays an active role in modifying proposals. It is true that certain public expenditure bills introduced by the executive, especially the budget, are passed virtually unmodified. The only significant modification of the 1970 Budget Bill, for instance, consisted of the deletion of a clause allowing the executive to take certain lands and buildings for the purposes of expanding the state-controlled television channel. In fact, this budget was dispatched by Congress in about four hours. Furthermore, even when the Congress does modify a budget, the executive often reverses such action via decree, as when the Minister of *Hacienda* ("Finance") issued a decree (Decree No. 388, February 1964) restoring the original level of the legislative budget, which had been lowered by Congress.

But is is unusual for the Congress to play such a mild modification role. In fact, with the exception of such projects as the budget, municipal loans, and *leyes de gracia*,[8] virtually all bills receive some, and in most instances, quite substantial, modification. (Even the municipal loans and *leyes de gracia* sometimes are amended.) For instance, in the 1963 regular legislature, we found only nine projects of significance which were able to get through any stage without modification, and many of these were probably changed during some later part of the legislative process. Again, in the 1964-65 extraordinary session, only three significant projects and only 26 bills passed the first discussion phase unchanged.

Of course, not all modifications are significant. Some involve only minor changes or insignificant altering of title orders. However, it appears that most changes are important ones. Of 70 projects analyzed in the 1962, 1963, 1965, and 1966 ordinary legislatures, 46 (65.7 percent) were significantly modified and 24 (34.3 percent) received only minor modifications. Unfortunately, these projects were of both executive and legislative origin, and we were not able to so divide them. However, it appeared from readings of the *Diarios de Sesiones* of the Congress that executive proposals were as likely as legislative ones to be significantly amended. We also collected some data on the 1963-64 and 1965-66 extraordinary legislatures to test this assumption. Of the 48 bills analyzed, 29 (60.4 percent) were significantly modified and 19 (39.6 percent) were modified only to a minor extent.

In some instances, the Congress has so modified a bill as to, in effect, completely rewrite it. One senator, replying to a press article criticizing the slowness with which Congress dispatched the projects before it for consideration, commented, "I would be able, in these instances, to indicate many laws that have been totally changed by the Congress" (Diario, 1966: 386). The senator then went on to note that most of these were necessary in order to improve a bill too hastily drawn up by the executive. While this type of modification has not been used with great freqeuncy, it has occurred often enough that an executive cannot simply paste together a bill and expect the legislature to meekly enact it.

Nor does the president's urgency power reduce congressional

influence in the modification stage. In Chile, the executive may request the legislature to apply an urgency classification to any project, thus, theoretically, requiring the chamber to dispatch the bill within a very limited time period (about twenty days). Although originally intended to be utilized for bills of utmost importance and requiring quick passage, this classification has been requested by the executive for a very large majority of his proposals. Because almost all of these requests are accepted by the legislature, it would appear that the time allotted to Congress to amend legislation would be severely limited. Such, however, is by no means always true (see also Agor, 1971b: 8-9, 10-15).

In May of 1962, Alessandri introduced one of his most important projects to Congress. This was a bill to modify the regulations concerning agrarian expropriations, farm sizes, and so on. It was, in fact, the most significant agrarian reform bill submitted to that date. At the time of the initiation of the bill, the President requested and received an urgency classification. Yet it was the end of July before both chambers approved the project in general[9] and early November before it was finally dispatched —significantly amended. Similarly, Frei's Copper Bill, introduced in late 1964, met with such opposition that Congress forced him to withdraw the *urgencia.* Once again, the legislature deliberated at great length and did not pass the bill until March 31, 1966.

The Chilean legislative system, much like that in the United States, is composed of important and hardworking standing committees. While it is not unusual for a bill to be amended on the floor, most of the work is done within the committees (see Agor, 1971b: 14). A high degree of committee autonomy and a high sense of duty and expertise make for a system in which much deliberation is devoted to bills. A combination of long hours of detailed deliberation and a multiparty representation on committees creates a situation whereby bills, especially important ones, tend to be modified. Thus such crucial bills as Alessandri's Agrarian Reform Bill and Frei's 1969 Constitutional Reform project spent long days in committee and emerged significantly amended.

For Chile, we may develop an additional index of policy dominance on the modification stage because the executive may also directly amend legislation by sending to Congress a series of "indications." Because there are so many executive indications proposed in any legislative session, we took a random sample of such proposals for the 1963 and 1966 ordinary legislatures and the 1964-65 extraordinary legislature to test the rate of acceptance.

As the data in Table 3 illustrate, the executive has been quite successful in gaining support for its amendments. With the exception of the 1963 Senate, a majority of all executive-proposed amendments have been

Table 3. Acceptance rate of executive amendments

	Chamber		Senate		Total	
	N	%[a]	N	%	N	%
1963	(34)	75.6	(22)	44.0	(56)	58.9
1964-1965	(62)	73.8	(72)	67.9	(113)	66.8
1966	(34)	82.9	(37)	78.7	(71)	80.7

a. Percentages based on total proposals for each chamber for that year

Source: Diario de Sesiones del Senado and Cámara, 1963, 1964-65, 1966.

---

accepted by the Congress. It is also interesting to note that Frei had greater success in this area than did Alessandri. We will attempt to explain this at the end of the section. For now, we merely note that not only does the Congress exert influence during the modification stage, but so too does the executive. In fact, it would appear that while congressional influence over policy-making reaches its zenith during this stage, its influence is then contained because the executive branch may successfully counter with its amendments. In any event, both branches actively participate in modifying policy proposals.

POLICY ACCEPTANCE OR REJECTION

While the Congress exerts quite strong influence in the areas of policy initiation and modification, it is completely dominated by the executive in acceptance-rejection. Overall approval rates for the 1961-1969 period varied from a low of 57 percent to a high of about 90 percent with a mean rate of about 80 percent. While no data exist which break down approval rates by source of initiation, case studies and other information (see Tapia, 1960: 38; and Olavarría, 1966: 387ff.) indicate that a higher percentage of presidential than congressional proposals are enacted. Furthermore, data for the 1967-68 extraordinary legislature, during which time all bills were, in effect, executive ones, show no rejections.

Although it is clear that the executive's leverage at this stage is much greater than the legislature's, it is difficult to ascertain whether or not there has been a trend toward greater executive dominance. The lack of data concerning the success of legislatively versus presidentially initiated legislation makes it virtually impossible to be certain about such developments. We can note a modest trend in terms of the overall rate. The percentage of bills approved by the Congress rose from 73 percent during the last four Alessandri years to 77 percent during the first five Frei years. In any event, it is clear that the executive has established dominance over this stage of policy-making.

POLICY REVIEW

The Congress also tends to be dominated by the executive on the review stage. Although the Chilean Congress has a number of resources at its disposal for the purpose of overseeing the executive branch, these are rarely used effectively enough to achieve this purpose. One organism most commonly cited which allows the Congress to oversee the executive is the office of the comptroller. While congressmen do receive information from this agency, which the comptroller general must furnish upon request, they rarely use it to alter executive behavior regarding the administration of legislation. To a very great extent this is because the control that may be exercised by the *Contraloría* is rather superficial and juridical (see Recabarren, 1969: 24; and Bulnes, 1967: 92-93). Thus, if this agency declares an executive decree "illegal," the president may overrule by a decree of insistence, which is basically a reissuing of the same decree signed by the chief executive and all the ministers. When this happens, the *Contraloría* reports to the Congress which then may take action, such as a constitutional accusation, but rarely does so.

Additionally, the Office of Information staffs of both chambers are not large enough for this function and are more involved in internal congressional business than in overseeing the executive branch. Consequently, the legislature does not have sufficient personnel to effectively and consistently oversee the administration. In fact, this lack of oversight activities is a constant complaint of congressmen. Typical is the response of one Christian Democratic deputy who commented to us that "in general, little outside fiscalization—of true import—is done with regard to the executive. What there is, is usually carried out by leftist parties for political purposes" (Interview, December 8, 1970).

On the other hand, one must be careful not to overemphasize executive freedom in its administration. At least sporadically, the legislature, particularly members of the partisan opposition, audits administrative behavior. Furthermore, a very highly developed and politicized communications network in Chile allows various groups to publicize administrative misbehavior to a highly politicized electorate. Congress may also question ministers in committee or on the floor and establish special investigating committees. The Left has used these devices on several occasions to inquire into government patronage, investigate housing failures, and so on. For instance, the Chamber established a special investigative commission to study the reasons for building failures during the 1965 earthquakes. The result was an accusation against a PDC deputy, severe embarrassment for the Christian Democrats, and a review of building policies (see Olavarría, 1966: 58, 61).

Finally, congressmen may perform both formal and informal oversight functions through their continual involvement in local government. Congressmen as key party members and local influenctials have great access to and leverage upon local administrators. Thus, while Congress may exert little direct leverage on administrative behavior, individual congressmen often do at the local level.

POLICY AS EXECUTIVE DECREES

Our analysis of policy dominance on the four stages of the policy process has shown a rather mixed picture. While it is clear that the executive dominates the acceptance-rejection and review stages, it would appear that the two branches are about equal in terms of policy initiation and modification. With regard to total output of policy, where we include executive decrees, we again return to a situation of executive dominance.

As the data in Table 4 indicate, the executive has consistently produced more policy decisions in the form of purely executive decisions than the legislature has in conjunction with the executive. Furthermore, there appears to be a strong trend in the direction of greater executive output. In the time period for which data was gathered (1959 to 1968), the quantity of executive decisions was initially higher than the legislature's by a 5.23:1 ratio, and then rose to 38 times that of the legislature in 1967, falling to a ratio of 15.20:1 in 1968.

The data on the quality of output are less precise, but once again give the edge to the executive. In terms of "legislative decisions," we would classify about 85 percent as unimportant. Of all laws enacted between 1959 and 1968, 61.5 percent were *leyes de gracia* (see Table 5), the vast majority of which do no more than grant small to moderate pensions to individual persons. Approximately 18 percent more have to do with municipal loans, freeing items from custom duties, and changing street and school names. Another category of minor laws includes those allowing for the erection of public monuments and those that simply clarify the texts of previous laws, about another 5 percent.[10]

Table 4. Ratio of executive to legislative output, 1959-1968

	1959[c]	1960	1961	1962	1963
Executive Output[a]	2334	2759	2833	2795	2838
Legislative Output[b]	446	515	451	286	330
Ratio	5.23	5.36	6.28	9.77	8.60
	1964	1965	1966	1967	1968
Executive Output	3416	3736	4871	4509	4679
Legislative Output	498	520	203	118	308
Ratio	6.86	7.18	24.00	38.21	15.20

    a. Executive output equals the total of all decrees and resolutions.
    b. Legislative output is the total number of laws (leyes).
    c. Year=administration years, i.e., from November of previous year through October of present year.

Source: Diario Oficial, 1959-1969

Table 5. Percentage of Leyes de Gracia *to total laws*

	1959[a]	1960	1961	1962	1963
Total Laws	446	515	451	286	330
Total Leyes de Gracia	283	326	292	166	182
Percentage	63.5	63.3	64.7	56.3	55.2
	1964	1965	1966	1967	1968
Total Laws	498	520	203	118	308
Total Leyes de Gracia	361	399	71	20	160
Percentage	72.5	76.7	35.0	16.9	51.9

    a. Years equal administration years, i.e., from November of previous year through October of present year.

Source: Diario Oficial, 1959-1969.

On the other hand, the ratio of important to unimportant decisions is not significantly greater for the executive. For instance, many executive decrees and resolutions do no more than reform the statutes of private companies. Another large body of executive decisions deals with administrative appointments. However, the significantly greater quantity of executive decisions means that a greater number of people and resources are affected than those affected by legislative decisions. This is particularly true when we recognize the limited influence that Congress has with regard to budgetary decisions.

AN OVERVIEW AND AN ATTEMPT AT EXPLANATION

The description of the relative policy positions of the executive and legislature has highlighted three principal developments. First, we have noted the overall position of dominance enjoyed by the executive. This is most particularly true in the areas of total output, acceptance-rejection, and policy review. Second, while the data were not conclusive on this point, there does seem to be a trend toward greater executive dominance. Third, we have suggested that, although the executive does have more control over decision-making, he cannot run roughshod over or completely dominate the legislature. Congress' highly active role in modifying presidential proposals and initiating its own proposals allows this institution its share of influence in decision-making. In the remainder of this section, we attempt to explain these trends and variations.

State Intervention in the Economy: Managerial Policy-Making

The first part of the analysis is a discussion of Beer's hypothesis and its utility in understanding the executive-legislative policy relationship in Chile. However, as Beer's hypothesis is really only concerned with one dimension of the decisional positions, we then must find other variables to account for changes in dominance on other dimensions. Here we will look at such factors as party opposition and public support for the two institutions.

As discussed previously, Beer (1966: 33-35) hypothesizes that as governments increase their intervention or influence upon the socioeconomic systems of their respective societies, the executive will tend to exert greater dominance in the making of policy decisions vis-a-vis the legislature. Hence, we must first ascertain the nature of executive intervention in Chile.

In Table 6 are presented three specific indicators of state intervention: total public expenditures, expenditures for salaries, and welfare

Table 6. Index of governmental intervention, 1959-1967[a]

Administration	Total Expenditures	Salaries	Welfare
Allessandri (1959-64)	4406.0	881.8	1150.3
1959	3752.9	621.4	649.4
1960	5233.4	713.2	1058.4
1961	4033.5	969.8	1251.7
1962	4579.5	1034.4	1507.7
1963	4255.6	967.1	1225.7
1964	4580.8	984.8	1208.8
Frei (1965-70)	7068.9	1338.6	1623.8
1965	5991.1	1146.2	1472.2
1966	7064.6	1330.2	1690.6
1967	8150.6	1539.3	1708.6

[a] Index derived by dividing actual expenditures by Consumer Price Index, dropping last three decimal places.

Source: Steven W. Sinding, "Political Participation, Government Expenditures and Economic Growth in Chile," (Unpublished Ph.D. Dissertation, University of North Carolina, 1970), pp. 225-228

spending. As can be readily seen from this table, the trend is fairly consistent toward higher governmental economic and social involvement.

According to Beer, two phenomena should be related to this development. One is an increase in decisions of a managerial type, that is, ones that are specific, technical and complex. Because, as a result of manpower, technical proficiency, and the like, the executive is better equipped to handle managerial decisions than the legislature, the second pehnomenon is a decrease in legislative output, a rise in the executive's output, and thus a rise in relative dominance of the latter. Let us look at these separately.

The graph in Figure 1 depicts the close fit between state intervention[11] and the ratio of executive to legislative output. In fact, only in the 1960-61 and 1963-64 periods do the two lines in the graph diverge. The closeness of association of the two variables is confirmed by a product-moment correlation coefficient of .87. At this level then, Beer's hypothesis seems to be well confirmed.

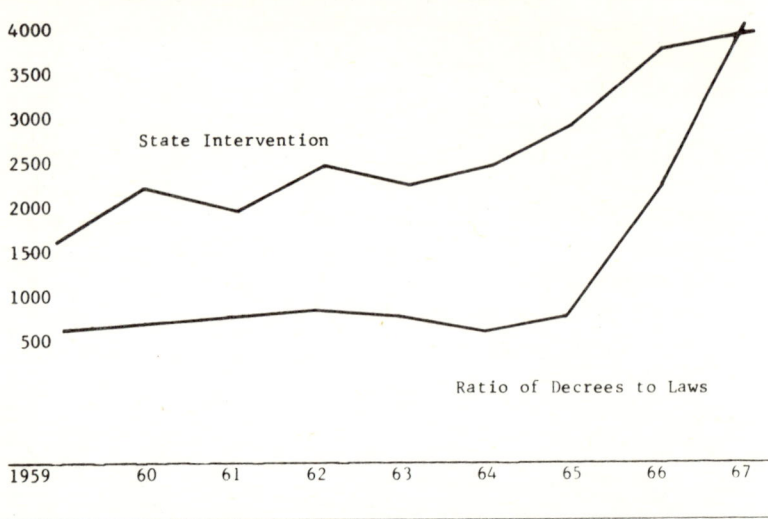

Figure 1. Relationship of state intervention to ratio of executive-legislative output (X 100), 1959-1967.

The second part of this hypothesis is the relationship between state intervention and decision type (managerial versus nonmanagerial) and the latter and executive-legislative output. As mentioned above, we were unable to satisfactorily operationalize all the components of this managerial-nonmanagerial variable; however, we were able to classify bills in terms of their scope. Because Beer (1966: 34) emphasizes the importance of the "increasing specificity of the essential governmental decision" in his definition of managerial policy, scope may well be a sufficient criterion for classifying. Thus we operationalized this variable by regarding national and regional decisions as nonmanagerial and local or individual decisions as managerial. Looking at the years 1959, 1962, and 1966, we found no clearly discernible trend. The percentage of laws classified as managerial declined slightly from about 72 percent in 1959 to 69 percent in 1962 but then rose again to about 71 percent in 1966.

Not only do these figures indicate a lack of a trend away from specific decision-making by the Congress, but they also indicate that a very high percentage of all congressional decisions are specific. In fact, a large part of the laws passed by the Congress today can be implemented without any recourse to the ordinance power of the President (see Cumplido, 1970: 37). If we add to this the fact that a great many of the amendments of Congress are also quite specific in scope, then it is even more apparent that the Chilean Congress plays a significant role in the making of managerial decisions.

On the other hand, the executive still plays the dominant role regarding specific decisions. Virtually all decrees and resolutions fit the definition of specific, managerial policies. Given the greater volume of decrees than laws, as well as a definite trend toward a higher ratio of decrees to laws, it seems accurate to state that the executive's relative dominance has increased because of a rise in specific decisions. The fact that the Chilean Congress exerts more leverage in the policy-making process than, say, the British Parliament may result in significant measure from the Chilean legislature's greater role in the shaping of specific decisions.

Party System: Opposition and Cohesion

While the variables of state intervention and specific policies go a long way toward explaining policy dominance in Chile, we still need to account for the variation not explained. Furthermore, why, if levels of state intervention have been so steadily and rapidly rising, has the Chilean Congress continued to play such a role in the making of specific decisions?

One variable that might account for variations in decisional dominance is the party system. In addition to state intervention and managerial policies, Beer (1966: 32-33) also concludes that a two-party system with very high party cohesion weakens the policy role of Parliament. Thus the nature of the party system may be an important factor in understanding Chilean executive-legislative relations.

Under the 1925 Constitution, Chilean laws provide for proportional representation. As Silvert (1961: 27) aptly describes the results, this situation has led to "one of the most stable multi-party systems in Latin America" with wide-ranging political representation. This in turn translates into broad congressional representation hampering the ability of any one party to dominate. In the 1958-1970 period, the number of parties in congress varied from twelve (1957-1961) to seven (1969-1973).

Throughout the years 1958-1970, at least one chamber was always controlled by the opposition. In the Alessandri years (1958-1964), the administration never had majority support in either chamber. Allessandri's congressional support came from the Conservatives, Liberals, and a fraction of the Radicals which joined the Frente Democrático.[12] This totaled about 43 percent of the Chamber and 41 percent of the Senate in the first two years and 39 percent of both houses thereafter. President Eduardo Frei's party support may be defined in terms of the support received by his own party, the Christian Democrats (Partido Democrata Christiano, PDC). In the first few months of Frei's administration, the PDC controlled only 19 percent of the seats in the Chamber of Deputies and 8 percent in the Senate. From 1965 to 1969, Frei had a majority in the lower house with 56 percent of the seats but controlled only 29 percent in the upper house. For the last year of this government, the party controlled 37 percent and 46 percent of the seats, respectively. Only, then, during the 1965-1969 years, did the administration have a majority in at least one chamber of Congress.

There was also a difference between Alessandri's and Frei's congressional support in terms of party cohesion. Not only did Frei experience greater numerical control of Congress but also his party exhibited higher levels of discipline. Based on 110 roll-call votes from 1958 to 1969, the index of party cohesion for the PDC was 93 while for the parties supporting Alessandri the overall index was about 81—81 for the Liberals, 91 for the Conservatives, and 72 for the Radicals (for a discussion of the index, see Anderson, Watts and Wilcox, 1966: 32-35). Viewed from another perspective, the degree of cohesion for the opposition parties was higher during Alessandri's administration. The bulk of his opposition came from the parties with the highest discipline: the Communists with a cohesion index of 99, the Socialists with 98, and the PDC (which during that period was closer to the Communists level of cohesion).

What then is the relationship between party support and the dominance positions? Our data indicate that there is an important relationship on four dimensions of policy dominance: total output, initiation, modification, and acceptance-rejection.

In terms of policy output, the correlation coefficient between the number of seats held by the government party and output (ratio of executive to legislative output) is .20. While this correlation is low, it is high enough to indicate a potentially important relationship. Further support of this is indicated by the fact that Frei dramatically increased the ratio of executive to legislative output precisely at the time he received a majority in the lower house (see Table 4). And he accomplished this through both an increase in executive output *and* a decrease in the quantity of legislative decisions.

A similar situation also developed in terms of initiation. The data in Table 2 indicate that both branches of government reduced the number of bills initiated during Frei's tenure and, what is perhaps more significant, reduced the quantity of important bills. This reduction is important because, as a study by Blondel (1969-70: 85) concludes, "the measurement of the superiority of the status of the government in relation to the Chamber is strongly correlated with the extent to which it can remain free not to present to the legislature more than a specified amount of important bills." Of course, these data do not prove that party support was responsible for these changes; however, they do certainly lend some credence to that hypothesis.

More demonstrable is the relationship between party support and success on roll-call votes. (These votes refer to amendments offered by the respective presidents.) On a total of 48 roll calls, Alessandri won on 34 of 70 (48 percent) while Frei won on 45 of 61 (75.4 percent). The difference in the overall levels of party support (combining both houses) was about 9 percent. Interviews and case studies also tend to confirm the hypothesis that party support is strongly related to executive dominance on the modification and acceptance-rejection dimensions.

In an interview (November 1970) with a member of the Senate Staff, we were told that the "system of political parties, their pluralism, plays an important role" in executive-legislative relations. This party pluralism means "that all [governmental] measure are the result of a game of conciliation of interests, a kind of give and take." A member of Congress similarly responded by saying that the "two most important factors regarding legislative-executive relations are the intervention of the state in economic matters and the regime of parties. For instance, President Frei always had difficulties with the Senate due to a lack of a majority" (Interview, December 1970).

A peculiarity in the amending process makes strong congressional support, in at least one chamber, even more important to the executive. This peculiarity concerns the process of insistence. In essence, insistence works as follows: Assume a bill originated in the Chamber. The Chamber approves the bill as initiated and sends it to the Senate. The Senate, by majority vote, amends the bill and returns it to the Chamber. The Chamber, again by a simple majority, rejects the Senate amendments. Now, in order for the Senate to insist in its modifications, it must muster a two-thirds vote. During Alessandri's administration, the government party had to allow many of its proposals to be amended because it did not have a majority and, frequently, could not even hold a one-third vote to reject insistences. Frei, on the other hand, had a majority in the Chamber and could usually control one-third of the Senate. Thus, even though Frei's proposals might be initially modified in the Senate, his party strength in the Chamber could force a vote of insistence, a vote the Senate could rarely muster.

Perhaps the most noteworthy example of this occurred during the legislative battle over Frei's Copper Bill. In order to ensure the bill's passage (and to ensure passage of his Agrarian Reform Bill), Frei allowed conservatives in the Senate to amend certain sections. But when the modified bill returned to the Chamber, the amendments were rejected. When the Senate then attempted to insist on its alterations, the Right could not hold the necessary two-thirds vote. Thus the bill was passed by the Congress in virtually the same form in which it had been initiated. This feat was achieved largely because of strong party support—and a little deception.

In Beer's discussion of the British Parliament and Wahl's (1966: 49-64) of the French legislature, two factors are consistently emphasized to explain the relative decisional positions of the executive and legislature: (1) the increasing role of the administration in managing the economy, and (2) the role of political parties. In both France and Great Britain, the first factor has diminished congressional influence over policy.

The second factor, political parties, may either hinder or promote executive dominance depending on the structure of the party system and the cohesiveness of the parties. Two-party systems where the executive has a well-disciplined majority (as in Britain) will increase executive dominance. The existence of a vital multiparty system with well-disciplined parties, such as those found in Chile and Fourth Republic France, will tend to decrease executive dominance, unless the executive can manage a majority.

Conceptually then, the party variable becomes a control variable vis-a-vis the state intervention-relative dominance relationship. State intervention generally tends to increase, and almost inevitably leads to an increase in, executive policy dominance. But the extent to which that relationship holds and the extent to which only slight increases in intervention might lead to larger increases in executive dominance depend, to a significant degree, on the party factor.

Over time, the relationship between state intervention and party support and the ratio of decrees to laws are strongly positive. Thus, while there was a continuing increase in the levels of state intervention throughout this period, Frei achieved substantially more dominance in policy-making, especially in quantity of important decisions and success of executive amendments. To a large extent, this seems to be accounted for by the fact that Frei had a majority (and a well-disciplined one) in one chamber while Alessandri never did.

Public Support

Within the focus on Chile, we observed one final factor that seemed to play a part in determining executive policy dominance. This factor concerns elite and mass support (or legitimacy) for the roles to be played by the executive and legislature in making policy. While little empirical research has been undertaken on this subject, there is enough evidence available to posit the relationship.

One of the primary reasons for the collapse of the Parliamentary Republic in Chile (1891-1925) was the withdrawal of public, and most particularly, elite (for example, military) support for the regime in general and for Parliament in particular. In the period since then, it appears that Congress has regained a good deal of lost support. Certainly during the Radical presidencies (1938-1952) much of the elite aligned itself with the Congress as a counterweight to the executive. More recently, however, there appears to be an increasing demand for a stronger executive voice in policy-making (see Piedrabuena, 1970: 55-59). A 1965 survey in Santiago by Eduardo Hamuy sought to elicit opinions concerning presidential versus congressional support in a situation of conflict between the two. While only 3 percent of the respondents thought the President should resign, almost 37 percent favored dissolving Congress (cited in Agor, 1971: 22-23). Various members of Congress, in interviews, commented on a growing dissatisfaction of the public regarding the legislature's influence in decision-making. In addition, these legislators were concerned that a significant segment of the public felt that this legislative influence impeded "proper" economic development and planning. Moreover, it is probably no accident that a constitutional reform measure was passed by Congress, restricting its own powers, precisely at a time when public support for Congress seemed to be on the wane.

This evidence is not, of course, proof of a direct relationship between popular support and policy dominance. We, therefore, must leave this as no more than a hypothesis. However, we do feel that what little information exists argues strongly in favor of considering public support levels as a type of contextual variable which, in conjunction with the Constitution, tends to place certain limits on the amount of policy influence available to either governmental institution.

COSTA RICA

METHODS AND PROCEDURES

The greater part of the data reported here were collected in Costa Rica from June through August of 1970. The primary data source was the archives of the Costa Rican Legislative Assembly where relatively complete information is filed on every bill that comes before the Assembly. The population examined was all bills initiated and resolved over a twelve-year period which encompasses the administrations of three presidents: Mario Echandi (1958-1962), Francisco Orlich (1962-1966), and José Joaquín Trejos (1966-1970).

The method of data storage in the archives was such that two samples rather than one had to be taken from two subpopulations. One subpopulation was all bills passed by the legislature which either became laws or were vetoed by the President of the Republic. A random sample, by year, was drawn from this subpopulation (n = 203). A similar sample was taken (n = 134) from the other subpopulation which consisted of all bills that had been defeated by the Legislative Assembly. Combining these two we have a total sample size of 337.

The combining of samples presented some problems, the crucial one being the ratio of bills passed to bills defeated. We were able to obtain figures on this variable ratio for the entire population. We constructed Table 7 by taking the average of bills in our sample defeated in each presidential administration and comparing that figure with a comparable statistic for the population as a whole.

Table 7. Proportion of bills that were defeated (by administration)

Administration	Sample	Population
Echandi	.450	.337
Orlich	.357	.357
Trejos	.354	.341

Only the Orlich administration displays a perfect sample-population fit on this dimension with slight oversampling of defeated bills characterizing the other administrations. Our conviction is that the degree of oversampling that does exist will not seriously bias the data analysis. Nevertheless, the reader should be aware of the discrepancies that do exist.

POLICY INITIATION

Christopher Baker (1971), in his study of the Costa Rican Legislative Assembly, found that, over a seven-month period (May through November of 1968), the legislature initiated 63 percent of all bills on the legislative docket, only 28 percent having been submitted by the executive (the remaining 9 percent were privately sponsored bills).[13] Moreover, if we consider private bills as essentially legislative bills, the Assembly achieved relative dominance over the executive by initiating almost three-fourths of all bills. Is there support for Baker's findings over a relatively longer time period? Over the twelve-year period examined here, there was evidence of legislative dominance in policy initiation (see Table 8).[14] Including private bills as legislative bills, the Legislative Assembly accounted for 64.1 percent of all bills submitted to the docket between 1958 and 1970. This

Table 8[15] *Initiator of bill*

Legislature	158 (46.9%)
Executive	121 (35.9%)
Private	58 (17.2%)
Total	337

position of legislative dominance is clear in all three presidential administrations with the percentage of legislative-private bills being 64.4 percent during the Echandi administration, 60.2 percent during the Orlich administration, and 67.7 percent during the Trejos administration.

But this approach to relative dominance in policy initiation is in terms of quantity only. As discussed earlier in this essay, the quality dimension must also be considered. Referring again to Polsby's (1963) criteria of importance, we lacked adequate information for the last three criteria. Therefore, we tentatively relied on the first: how many people are affected by outcomes. This criterion was operationalized by the use of a national-local dichotomy. National bills presumably affect the totality of the population or a segment which cuts across parochial lines. Local bills affect only a local, parochial segment of the population. Hence, we are positing that, because of an avowedly broader impact, national bills are "more important" than local bills.

More than half of all policy-making by laws in Costa Rica in the period studies was of the national type. The legislature initiated a majority of these "important" bills and more than three-fourths of the local or "unimportant" bills (see Table 9). We conclude that the legislature occupies a position of relative dominance in the initiation of both national and local policy.

A second criterion suggested by Baker (1971) might also be used for judging the relative importance of bills. This criterion is committee assignment of bills and is based upon the notion that some committees are more important than others in that they deal with policies that are potentially more significant in distributing resources for society. Following Baker's procedure, we asked several legislative experts to rank the standing committees according to their relative importance.[15] With one

Table 9. Initiation of bills with national vs. local impact

	National	Local	Total
Legislature[a]	105 (52.8%)	110 (80.3%)	215
Executive	94 (47.2%)	27 (19.7%)	121
Total	199	137	336

$x^2 = 25.50 \quad p \leq .001$

[a] Unless otherwise noted, the tables include private bills in the legislative category.

---

exception, the rankings were highly consistent, although they differed from Baker's rankings in that the highest ranked committee in Baker's study occupied the number two spot in our research and vice-versa. In order of descending importance, we shall describe each committee in terms of the subjects of the bills normally assigned to each.

(1) *Comisión de Asuntos Hacendarios.* This committee deals exclusively with all national budget bills as well as with matters of taxation.

(2) *Comisión de Asuntos Económicos.* Somewhat broader than the previous committee, this one is normally assigned bills that deal with general economic affairs, foreign loans, Central American Common Market agreements, commerce, and industry.

(3) *Comisión de Gobierno y Administración.* This committee deals with governmental affairs, public security, foreign affairs of a largely noneconomic nature, public works projects, municipal affairs, and agriculture.

(4) *Comisión de Asuntos Sociales.* This committee is assigned all labor bills, social security measures and, broadly, all bills whose subject matter deals with health, education, and welfare.

(5) *Comisión de Asuntos Jurídicos.* All proposed constitutional amendments, civil, penal, procedural, administrative, and

electoral law and all other judicial matters make up the subject matter of this committee.

It should be pointed out that these are general rankings, because it was repeatedly pointed out to this researcher that there were a number of important exceptions to the general rule. For example, although the Comisión de Asuntos Sociales is ranked next to last in importance, the 1966 bill which became the 1968 Law of Cooperative Associations, considered to be an important national policy, was assigned to this committee where it received a unanimously favorable report.[16]

Two other caveats are also in order. First, prior to 1962, a different committee system existed with more than twice as many permanent committees. We classified these pre-1962 bills by subject matter and assigned them to the current committees on this basis. Second, a recent change in the internal regulations of the legislature gave the President of the Assembly the right to assign a bill to whichever committee he deems proper. If this prerogative was used loosely, this fact could cause a bias in our classification scheme. One ought to view Table 10 with these qualifications in mind.

With the exception of one committee, albeit an important one, the legislature maintains relative dominance in this dimension of importance also. If, however, we create a dichotomy where the two highest ranked committees are important and the three lowest are unimportant, then the executive gets the edge in the initiation of important policies. Taken as a whole, though, we may conclude that the Legislative Assembly is relatively dominant over the executive in the initiation stage of policy-making.

Table 10. Initiation of bills by committee assignment

Committee (In descending order of importance)	Legislature-initiated	Executive-initiated
Comision de Asuntos Hacendarios	18 (55.6%)[a]	16 (44.4%)
Comision de Asuntos Economicos	16 (40.0%)	24 (60.0%)
Comision de Gobierno y Administracion	53 (63.9%)	30 (36.1%)
Comision de Asuntos Sociales	26 (63.4%)	15 (36.6%)
Comision de Asuntos Juridicos	31 (79.5%)	8 (20.5%)

[a]These are row percentages.

POLICY MODIFICATION

The first aspect of this stage which is examined involves committee reports—affirmative or negative. Which is more successful, the legislature of the executive, in receiving affirmative committee reports on its bills? Table 11[17] shows the number and the percent of negative and affirmative committee reports given legislature-sponsored and executive-initiated.

Table 11. Committee reports on bills considered [18]

Sponsor of Bill	Affirmative Report	Negative Report	Total
Legislature	83 (76.2%)[a]	26 (23.8%)	109
Executive	64 (94.1%)	4 (15.9%)	68

$x^2 = 8.37$ $p \leq .01$

[a]These are row percentages.

While both the executive and the legislature received affirmative reports on the vast majority of bills each initiated, the executive is relatively dominant in that a significantly greater proportion of its bills are approved by all committees. At first glance, one is struck by the relative acquiescence of committees in the Assembly. Before drawing conclusions about this stage, it would be useful to examine the nature and degree of modification performed on those bills that do receive affirmative committee reports.

Of the 146 bills given an affirmative recommendation, 97 were either completely unchanged or only slightly modified, the great majority being in the former category (75 of 97 were not changed at all by the committees). Almost two-thirds of all committee-approved bills were virtually or completely unchanged. As Table 12 indicates, the executive still holds the edge over the legislature with almost three-fourths of its proposals being approved virtually unchanged. Even given this edge by the executive, the legislature fared almost as well with somewhat less than two-thirds of its bills receiving similar treatment by the committees. The legislature did suffer a greater portion of significant changes to its proposals than did the executive.

We also examined these dimensions of the modification stage by presidential administration and found virtually no variation between

Table 12. Committee modification of bills given affirmative committee reports.

Sponsor of Bill	Degree of Modification[19]		
	None to Slight	Moderate	Significant to Complete
Legislature	51 (61.5%)[a]	22 (26.5%)	10 (12.0%)
Executive	46 (73.0%)	14 (22.2%)	3 (4.8%)

$x^2 = 0.6 \; p \leq .40$

[a] These are row percentages.

administrations (see Tables 13 and 14). We had expected an increase in the role of committees in the modification of policies since 1962 because, as we mentioned earlier, the committee system underwent structural changes in that year which were intended to strengthen the position of committees in the policy-making process. Without exception,

Table 13. Committee decisions on bills considered (by administration)

Administration	Decision	Sponsor of Bill	
		Legislative-Private	Executive
Echandi	Affirmative	18 (58.3%)[a]	20 (41.7%)
	Negative	12 (92.3%)	1 (7.7%)
Orlich	Affirmative	27 (55.2%)	22 (44.8%)
	Negative	7 (87.5%)	1 (12.5%)
Trejos	Affirmative	28 (56.0%)	22 (44.0%)
	Negative	7 (77.8%)	2 (22.2%)

[a] These are row percentages.

Table 14. Committee modification of bills given affirmative committee reports (by administration)

Administration	Degree of Modification	Sponsor of Bill	
		Legislature-Private	Executive
Echandi	Insignificant[a]	28 (96.6%)[b]	20 (95.2%)
	Significant	1 (3.4%)	1 (4.8%)
Orlich	Insignificant	22 (84.6%)	21 (100%)
	Significant	4 (15.4%)	0 (0.0%)
Trejos	Insignificant	23 (82.1%)	20 (90.9%)
	Significant	5 (17.9%)	2 (9.1%)

[a] None to slight and moderate were combined to form this category.

[b] These are column percentages computed by administration.

former legislators interviewed by the author asserted that committees have had much more influence over the fate of a bill since the committee reform which went into effect in May of 1962. Our data cast doubt on their evaluation. Post-1962 committee modifications show no variation from pre-1962 decisions. Obviously, the supposed strengthening of the committees through structural change has not manifested itself in a greater tendency to modify bills. Nor was there a greater propensity after 1962 for committees to reject proposals by giving them negative reports.

A general conclusion is that neither the executive nor the legislature is really dominant in terms of policy modification, nor is there any clear trend in one direction or the other. The legislature submits the majority of all bills given an affirmative committee report and approved with little or no modification, but the executive does not go below the 40 percent mark in these same categories. Moreover, although the executive accounts for a smaller obsolute number of bills reported out of committee, it is more successful than the legislature *in relative terms* in achieving a better approval-disapproval record in committee and a somewhat better ratio of unchanged bills. Furthermore, committees, in playing only a minor role in modification of policy proposals, have little significantly effect on the relative dominance of the executive vis-a-vis the legislature.

A final aspect of the modification stage involves the role of the entire Legislative Assembly and focuses on policy changes that are made between the final committee report and the final voting decision of the whole Assembly. As discussed previously, measurement of relative dominance in this phase may turn out to be less clear-cut than in the previous policy modification phase because legislative approval, disapproval, and/or modification may be attributed to intra-legislative struggle as well as to executive-legislative relations. This should not be a problem for those bills that bypassed the committee phase of the process.

Except for the fact that the legislative bills make up the greatest number of bills passed by the Assembly, there is once again no indication of relative dominance by either institution. As Table 15 shows, however, the executive did have the only bills in the sample which were significantly changed by the legislature. In all, 165 of 200 bills passed by the Legislative Assembly were completely unchanged from the committee version, which leads perhaps too easily to a "rubber stamp" interpretation of the impact of the whole legislature upon policy proposals. It should be remembered, however, that not all bills are passed. The situation in Costa Rica is both similar to and distinct from that in Great Britain where

Table 15. Assembly modification of bills[a]

Sponsor of Bill	Degree of Modification	
	Insignificant[b]	Significant
Legislature	112 (100%)[c]	0 (0.0%)
Executive	85 (96.6%)	3 (3.4%)

$x^2 = 1.09$ $p \geq .30$

[a] Excludes defeated bills

[b] None to slight, and moderate were combined to form this category; the significant category also includes those bills that were completely changed.

[c] These are row percentages.

Bernard Crick argues that all important (that is, Government) legislation "goes through [Parliament] without substantial amendment" (1970: 51-52). In Costa Rica both Government (executive) and congressional legislation is insignificantly modified, but *only to the extent that it passes*.

POLICY ACCEPTANCE OR REJECTION

Of 137 bills that were defeated, more than 76 percent were legislature-initiated (including private bills), giving the executive a relative position of dominance in this regard. There is also little variation across administrations, as Table 16 demonstrates. Moreover, a greater percentage of legislature-initiated bills are defeated than are executive-initiated bills, with an overall defeat-to-passage ratio of .93 for the former compared to a ratio of .38 for that latter.[19] The executive seems to occupy a clear position of relative dominance in all time periods.

Table 16. Bills defeated (by administration)

Sponsor of Bill	Echandi	Orlich	Trejos
Legislature	42 (76.4%)	30 (71.4%)	31 (79.5%)
Executive	13 (23.6%)	12 (28.6%)	8 (20.5%)
TOTAL	55	42	39

$x^2 = .254$ $p \leq .90$

To amplify, and perhaps modify, this view somewhat, we should examine more carefully the notion of defeat in the Costa Rican context. In one sense a bill defined as a policy proposal may never actually be defeated because it can be reintroduced again and again, albeit within certain restrictions and time period limitations.[20] Even if a bill is defeated by majority vote in one of the three legislative floor debates, it can be reintroduced in the next legislative calendar year. A presidential veto may not really be final, because what frequently occurs after a bill passed by the Assembly is vetoed is actually an ex post facto continuation of the bargaining or modification stage. The bill returns to the legislature along with the president's reasons for vetoing the bill, and his recommendations are frequently adopted, only to return once again for the presidential endorsement.[21]

In this light, the notion of defeat becomes more slippery. For the purposes of this study, then, defeat means being held up for two years in committee and/or on the floor (because a two-year time limit is assigned to all bills), being shuffled between the floor and committees for more than two years, or receiving an outright negative vote in one of the three floor debates. In this regard, the executive is relatively dominant vis-a-vis the legislature because a greater proportion of its proposals are passed. At the same time, it must be noted that the legislature initiated the majority of all bills that it eventually passed into law.

But let us briefly examine the qualitative dimension of policy importance during this decision stage. In keeping with our notion that national policies are more important than local ones, Table 17 indicates that the executive is dominant in the passage of national bills while the legislature is predominant in the number of "unimportant" bills accepted by the Legislative Assembly.

Table 17. *Sponsorship of bills accepted by the legislative assembly by policy type.*

Sponsor	Policy Type	
	National	Local
Legislature	39 (36.8%)	74 (78.7%)
Executive	67 (63.2%)	20 (21.3%)
TOTAL	106	94

$x^2 = 33.90 \ p \leq .001$

POLICY REVIEW

To what extent does the Legislative Assembly oversee executive agencies responsible for administering policy? We inquired of our group of experts (described in note 15): "Do you think it is the duty of the Legislative Assembly to oversee the actions of the ministers of the executive branch and the autonomous institutions?"

The responses were split almost evenly. The Liberación Nacional (PLN) deputies and ex-deputies, the majority party in the Assembly, with but one exception said that it is definitely the duty of the Assembly to keep tabs on the actions of the other branches of government. Non-PLN people, and one PLN deputy, agreed that oversight was a common practice of the legislature. They disagreed, however, that this was a correct procedure to follow. As one former Unión Nacional deputy put it, this power of oversight ". . . has been abused. From 1949 to the present [1970] the Assembly has been sticking its nose into places where it doesn't belong. These things are administrative problems, not legislative ones."[22]

What tools are available to the legislature to perform this function? All respondents pointed out that the Comptroller General of the Republic, an arm of the Legislative Assembly, was a powerful tool to utilize because it oversees the funding of all aspects of the national budget. Aside from this agency, the other means of oversight available to the Assembly carry little more "moral" persuasion. The Assembly issues what are called *excitativas*, which are not more than formal pleas to the executive or to an autonomous institute requesting that they change or implement some policy. They do not carry a binding sanction. The legislature also makes use of what Baker calls a very partisan tool: the ability to censure ministers of the executive. In 1968 an unsuccessful attempt was made to censure three ministers, one of whom was the son of the President of the Republic (Baker, 1971). Needless to say, the party in control of the legislature was not the President's party.

We lack systematic data regarding the application of these tools. Even though, theoretically, the Comptroller can oversee the manner in which the budget is spent, it is unclear how often he does so. More work needs to be done in this phase of the policy process before even tentative conclusions about relative dominance can be made.

POLICY AS EXECUTIVE DECREES

While Charles Denton (1971: 36) argues that the President of Costa Rica, unlike many other Latin American presidents, lacks a widespread decree authority, he overlooks the fact that the executive branch does issue numerous administrative decrees that have the force of law. While these decrees supposedly must be made within the scope of existing laws, they can still be conceived of as a form of policy-making enacted independently of direct interactions with the Legislative Assembly. Moreover, many of our experts pointed out several instances where decrees actually went beyond the scope of existing laws, at least in the perception of the legislature. The substance of these decrees varies all the way from bills that declare a National Day for typographical workers to those that modify segments of the national budget. In other words, decrees deal with many of the same policies that the legislature together with the executive deal with in the form of laws.

As Figure 2 indicates, in every year between 1962 and 1970 except one, there were more decrees issued by the executive than laws passed. Overall, about one and one-half times as many decrees as laws were passed in that time period. By and large, decrees are quite specific in their application, more so than many laws. This type of policy-making seems to be what Samuel Beer had in mind when he spoke of the contrast between "government by specific decision and government by general rules" (Beer, 1966: 34). On this dimension, the executive, acting independently of the legislature, is relatively dominant, at least in quantitative terms.

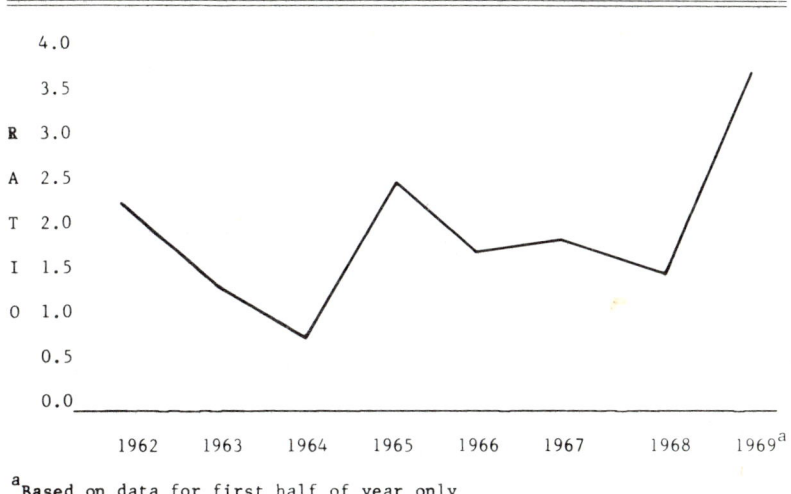

[a] Based on data for first half of year only

Figure 2. Ratio of decrees to laws (by year)

The use of decrees has additional implications for the review stage of the policy process. In the instances where the legislature perceives that the executive has stepped out of bounds, especially on highly public and controversial decrees, the tools of "moral persuasion" seem to be effective. For example, during the regime of President Echandi, a large workers' strike took place in the city of Puntarenas on the west coast. Echandi issued a decree prohibiting anyone from entering the area, including deputies of the Legislative Assembly. After much legislative outcry concerning the illegality of the decree, it was repealed.[23] But what about the hundreds of less public decrees issued each year? Our impression is that the great majority of executive decrees, regardless of their constitutionality, are not examined and reviewed by the legislature simply because of lack of time and lack of adequate research staff facilities. The decree, therefore, can be a powerful tool in asserting the relative dominance of the executive.

AN OVERVIEW AND AN ATTEMPT AT EXPLANATION

Without question, the legislature dominates the initiation stage of policy-making, both quantitatively and qualitatively. It initiated more bills, both "important" (national) and "unimportant" (local), than the executive in every year between 1958 and 1969 except one. Moreover, the historical pattern is one of cyclical increase, with the low points of legislative dominance becoming less deep and the high points becoming higher.

In terms of the modification stage, the executive is relatively more successful than the legislature in obtaining affirmative reports from committees. Although most bills given affirmative committee reports were left unchanged, the executive had fewer of its bills modified significantly than did the legislature. The legislature is anything but overwhelmed in this regard, however, with more than three-fourths of its bills being insignificantly modified. When we speak of modification in terms of how the final law resembles or differs from the original bill and/or the committee's version, we have a virtual toss-up between the executive and the legislature. Both are eminently successful in getting bills passed in largely unchanged form.

The only bills in our sample accepted by the Assembly were those that received affirmative committee reports. The committees take on more significance here in that a negative report appears to be the proverbial "kiss of death" for any and all policies that go on to the final acceptance-rejection stage. In this stage the executive clearly assumes a position of relative dominance in terms of the small proportion of its bills that suffer rejection. At the same time, the executive is busy issuing numerous decrees with little worry that they will be challenged by the legislature.

As is apparent, conclusions about relative dominance in the overall policy process are mixed, with neither the executive nor the legislature assuming a position of predominance. How, then, might we account for the variation that we do see? The remainder of this section will explore some of the factors mentioned previously in this essay, beginning with Beer's (1966) notion which links state intervention in the economy with managerial policies and, in turn, with executive dominance in policy-making.

State Intervention in the Economy: Managerial Policy-Making

The perspective of this notion involves the assertion that the complexities of modern life, hence of political life, are such that more demands are being made on the state for the solution of political, economic, and social problems. As the state then intervenes in these affairs, especially economic ones, the nature of the policies will become increasingly managerial; that is, they become specific, complex, and technical, requiring considerable expertise. The executive branch is seen as the one best equipped in terms of training, expertise, and ability to move rapidly. Jacques Lambert (1967) has hinted at a similar phenomenon in the context of Latin-American development.

Do we have any indication that the Costa Rican government has increased the role it plays in the economic life of the nation? One indicator might be the proportion of the country's gross national product (GNP) accounted for by the government. As Table 18 shows, while the government is still the smallest sector in the economy (at least through 1966), it is the only sector that has doubled its share of the GNP in a little over a decade. But these figures do not fully comprehend the government's role, for the government is defined in the table as the central government. If we were to include the autonomous and semi-autonomous agencies as well as local governments, we would then be speaking of the

Table 18. Makeup by sector of Costa Rican gross national product

Sector	1950	1955	1960	1963	1966
Agriculture	41%	35%	31%	29%	29%
Industry (manufacturing)	12	13	14	15	16
Commerce	14	15	14	14	14
Service	14	14	14	15	15
Government	5	8	9	10	9
Other (transportation, energy, housing)	14	15	18	17	17
TOTAL (GNP)	100%	100%	100%	100%	100%

SOURCE: Oficina de Planificación (1967: 4)

Table 19. Public sector income, gross national product, and public sector income as a percentage of GNP (in millions of colones)

Subsector	1968	1969
Central Government	748.6	941.6
Decentralized Organizations (autonomous and semi-autonomous institutions)	894.8	1,055.2
Local Administrations	48.8	50.1
TOTAL (public sector)	1,692.2	2,047.0
Gross National Product	5,063.9	5,588.9
Public Sector Income as a Percentage of Gross National Product	34.4%	36.6%

Sources: For public sector income, **Memoria Anual. Enero a Diciembre 1969**, Contraloría de la República (San José, 1970): for Gross National Product data, **Cifras económicas de Costa Rica**, Banco Central de la República (San José, 1969).

role of the total public sector in the nation's economy. As Table 19 indicates, the public sector's total income accounted for over one-third of the GNP in both 1968 and 1969. Moreover, in terms of the total public expenditures, there was a slight, though steady, increase in public expenditures as a portion of GNP from 1967 through 1969 (see Table 20).

Table 20. Public sector expenditures as a percentage of GNP (in millions of colones)

Year	Public Sector Expenditures	GNP	Public Sector Expenditures/GNP
1967	1,363.1	4,595.3	29.6%
1968	1,508.2	5,063.9	29.7
1969	1,750.1	5,588.9	31.3

Sources: For public sector expenditures, <u>Anuario estadístico</u>, Contraloría de la República (San José, 1969); for GNP, Banco Central, <u>ibid</u>.

From another angle, we can look at the percentages of the work force employed by the government. As Table 21 demonstrates, between 1950 and 1963 the government doubled the percentage of the national work force it employs, a growth rate unequalled by any other single sector. Charles Denton (1971: 19) provides us with a brief summation which points to the omnipresent role of the Costa Rican government in the nation's socioeconomic affairs:

> The government is a producer and owner not only of public services and utilities such as highways, hospitals, schools, and electric power facilities but also of consumer goods and services and industrial and commercial facilities. A government monopoly manufactures all alcoholic beverages produced in the country with the exception of beer. Government monopolies also own and operate a railway from the capital city of San José to the Pacific Ocean, the national banking system, the country's only insurance company, and its only petroleum refinery; the government is the principal shareholder of LACSA international airlines. One government institution not only finances the construction of housing for the poor, but also provides tools and materials, and in some cases builds the edifice.

Table 21. *Employment by sectors of economy in census years (percentage of work force)*

Sector	1927	1950	1963
Industry	8	11	12%
Agriculture and Fishing	62	55	49
Government	-	5	10
Commerce	6	8	7
Service	14[a]	15	17
Other	10	6	5
TOTAL	100	100	100%

[a] Includes government

Source: Charles F. Denton (1971:14).

Though the above data is limited in the sense that we have little precise notion of changes over time by year, it nonetheless seems suggestive of the kind of situation Beer (1966) had in mind when he spoke of increasing state intervention in the economy. Given this avowedly scanty yet suggestive data, we would expect the nature of governmental policy-making to be increasingly managerial in nature. One dimension of managerial policy-making is specificity. This dimension is emphasized by Beer when he speaks of "the increasing specificity of the essential governmental decision" (Beer, 1966: 34). In terms of laws, we conceptualized local policies as being essentially specific in application in that the target was usually a single individual or organization or region of the country rather than the country as a whole. Also, specific decisions tend to deal with a relatively limited point in time rather than being applicable across time.

From our previous discussions, we have seen that managerial policies defined as specific (local) laws have not resulted in increasing executive dominance in the initiation stage of the process. The opposite occurs where we see the legislature playing a significant role in the initiation of this type of policy. We see a similar lack of relative dominance of the executive in the modification stage dealing with managerial (local) bills. However, the edge that the legislature seems to have established in this regard is thwarted in the acceptance-rejection stage. The executive does a better job of getting its managerial policies accepted than does the legislature. Nonetheless, the legislature still accounts for the majority of all those managerial policies that are ultimately accepted by the whole legislature. Overall, Beer's notion does not appear to apply to Costa Rica.

On the other hand, we must consider another dimension of "managerialness": complexity and technicality. This dimension did not overlap with the other in its application to the sample of bills in Costa Rica. This concept was operationalized by using the author's "intuition" and "common sense" rather than by some fairly rigid empirical indicators. Following this procedure, we classified some 20 percent of the bills as technical, hence managerial. These bills, like those in the specificity category, display no systematic longitudinal increase in their proportion of all policies; this, of course, is not what we would have expected given Beer's notions. A major finding was that there was a positive relationship between technical policies and relative executive dominance in all stages of the policy process. In this regard, the technicality diminsion of managerial policies supports the relationships hypothesized by Beer. The executive initiated more than 65 percent (45 of 69) of all technical bills, received affirmative committee reports for 94.7 percent of those, and accounted for almost 83 percent of all managerial (technical) policies that eventually became law.

If we momentarily expand our notion of policy to include executive decrees once again, we will attempt to place decree-making into the context of Beer's hypothesis. We have already noted that decrees often perform the same task as laws. Moreover, it is possible that executives might use these decrees, most of which are managerial (in this instance, specific) in nature, to avoid the delays of dealing with law-making in light of the increase in state intervention in the economy. However, while we have already described the fact that decrees outnumber laws, as Figure 2 showed, there is no systematic increase over time in the use of decrees. While the data for 1969 show a marked rise in the issuance of decrees relative to laws, it must be remembered that the figure is based on the first half of the year only.[24] Later, we will return briefly to analyze decrees in terms of party opposition within the legislature.

Party Opposition

Party opposition, as discussed in the section on Chile, is generally seen as having something to do with the nature of the relationship between the executive and the legislature. Might this be true in Costa Rica? According to one observer of the Legislative Assembly, "party discipline is strictly enforced, and issues are sharply debated." (Denton, 1971: 36). Since legislators and the president of the Republic are elected simultaneously for a four-year period, party opposition, defined as seats held by non-administration parties in the legislature, remains constant within administrations. Therefore, we analyzed the effects of this factor between administrations rather than by year.

In formulating our measure of party opposition, we made a very critical assumption: that non-PLN (National Liberation Party) parties tend to band together against the PLN on particular issues and vice-versa. We therefore merely used the ratio of PLN to non-PLN members as a measure of party opposition. To be more exact, during the Echandi and Trejos administrations, which were both non-PLN, the proportion of seats held by the PLN served as our measure. In the Orlich administration, the proportion of non-PLN held seats was our measure.

Was the above assumption a valid one? Although the two main non-PLN parties, the National Republican Party (PRN) and the National Union Party (PUN), were bitter enemies during the 1948 Civil War, they have come to overlook their differences in an effort to block PLN programs and have formed the Party of National Unification. A statement from the secretary-general of the anti-PLN coalition during the Trejos administration lends credence to this interpretation:

We of the Unification, in essence, are those Costa Ricans who
are neither in agreement with the theses, procedures and points
of view of the National Liberation Party nor with the political
behavior of their leaders. [La Nación, September 4, 1970: 18].

Also, those minor parties represented in the legislative sessions during the
period of our research held no more than two seats in any given period.
Besides, these too could be generally classified as essentially anti-PLN
parties, particularly the Revolutionary Civic Union Party (UCR).

This definition of party opposition allowed us to construct a rank
ordering of presidential administrations according to their relative degrees
of party opposition. The orderings were very close with the Echandi
administration having a score of .44; the Orlich administration, .49; and
the Trejos administration, .51. As Table 22 demonstrates, the relationship
between party opposition and relative dominance in policy initiation is
insignificant.

Table 22. *Relationship between party opposition and relative dominance in policy initiation*

Degree of Party Opposition	Initiator of Bill	
	Legislature-Private	Executive
Low (Echandi)	78 (64.5%)[a]	43 (35.5%)
Medium (Orlich)	68 (60.2%)	45 (39.8%)
High (Trejos)	69 (67.7%)	33 (32.3%)

[a] These are row percentages
$X^2 = 2.412$
$p \leq .30$

Given the small differences among administrations in terms of the
party opposition score, this finding is not particularly surprising. However,
we would expect the party opposition variable, even given the closeness
of the three scores, to do a somewhat better job in accounting for relative
dominance in the modification and acceptance-rejection stages.

Looking at modification in terms of committee approval or disapproval, we calculated the mean executive dominance score within administrations (see Table 23). In this instance, reporting a measure of association would be extremely misleading given the very small number of cases. We note, however, that there does appear to be an inverse relationship between government party opposition and executive dominance as predicted.

Table 23. Party opposition and executive dominance in obtaining affirmative committee reports

Party Opposition Score	Executive Dominance in Obtaining Affirmative Committee Reports
.44	.24
.49	.20
.51	.13

Is there a relationship between the party variable and relative dominance in the acceptance-rejection stage? We would predict that the greater the party opposition, the greater the rate of defeat of bills initiated by the executive (that is, the less the relative dominance of the executive). We again averaged the proportion of executive-initiated defeated bills by administration so that we could compare this to the independent variable (Table 24).

Table 24. Relationship between party opposition and the rejection of executive bills

Administration	Party Opposition Score	Proportion of Rejected Bills That were Executive-Initiated (by administration)
1958-1961	.44	.207
1962-1965	.49	.448
1966-1969	.51	.219

We do not find the predicted relationship in this instance, the Trejos administration being the deviant case. One possible reason for the defiance of the last administration may be taken from some of Baker's

(1971) observations of the 1968 legislative term. During the Trejos administration, the PRN legislative caucus, one part of the Unification coalition, appeared to maintain a somewhat strained relationship with the executive branch. Consequently, little coordination was evident between the PRN legislative caucus and the executive in the case of executive-sponsored bills; the caucus members did not seem to view themselves as allies of the executive. Therefore, although the PLN was cast as the opposition party, one frequently saw PLN rather than administration party deputies playing the role of committee and floor defenders of executive bills.

We might also examine executive decrees in light of party opposition. Figure 2 displays data for two administrations: Orlich and Trejos. In eliminating 1962, which was actually Echandi's last year in office, we can obtain an average ratio score by administration of decrees to laws. The mean score for the Orlich administration, which enjoyed majority support in the Legislative Assembly, was 1.6. The score for the Trejos administration, which had only minority party support, was 2.4 if we include the data for 1969 which, as pointed out earlier, is only for a half year. Moreover the Trejos administration also had the Deputies who may only be elected for a four-year term with no immediate reelection. This prohibition would seem to work against the possibility of establishing meaningful subject matter expertise in the legislature. This lack of expertise and experience was probably manifested in our data when we observed that both the committees and the legislature as a whole were reluctant to offer modifications to any bills, but especially executive-initiated bills.

Two additional factors, one of them constitutional, might also help to explain the legislature's reluctance to modify executive bills. On some issues, such as budgetary matters, the legislature is required to seek the "expert advice" of the executive branch. Also, the committees lack full-time research staffs. What often occurs, therefore, is committee decision-making based almost entirely on testimony given by the same agency that originally sponsored the bill.

Insofar as we saw variations in relative dominance in the various policy stages, one is tempted to conclude that, at least in party, it is a result of the "intent of the framers." The fear of executive dominance seems to have combined with a fear of concentrating power in any branch of government which has resulted in a politics of mutual one-upsmanship in the policy process with neither branch either winning or losing.

COMPARING RELATIVE DOMINANCE IN CHILE AND COSTA RICA: SUMMARY AND CONCLUSIONS

Throughout this essay we have continually referred to the need to systematically conceptualize legislative-executive relationships in terms of relative dominance in the policy-making process. The intent has been to place the particular cases of Chile and Costa Rica in a broader, more comparative perspective. In the substantive sections of this paper, we applied these conceptual tools to our primary task of describing the relative dominance positions of the executive and the legislature in the various stages of the policy process. We also attempted to account for differences in relative dominance in policy-making.

The remainder of this essay will consist of two parts. The first will summarize as well as evaluate this effort to account for differences. This summary will include a tentative list of hypotheses suggested by the research findings. The second part will largely be used to suggest further avenues of research along the lines of this study.

ACCOUNTING FOR DIFFERENCES

From our discussions and analyses of Chile and Costa Rica, several factors have been suggested that seem to be important in determining the relative dominance positions of the executive and/or the legislature in the policy process. We shall limit our discussion, by and large, to those factors that appear to be common to both Chile and Costa Rica. These common factors are the nature of the constitutional system, state intervention in the economy, the managerial nature of governmental decision-making, and administration party opposition in the legislature.

We can now more systematically arrange these factors by the following set of hypotheses:

(1) The historical combination of constitutional regulations and constitutional observance will set the base level of legislative-executive relative dominance in policy-making such that:

  (1.1) Only in those systems which constitutionally sanction an active legislature and develop a history of constitutional observance will the legislature consistently play a role in decision-making, but

  (1.2) The extent to which it plays this role will be determined by other factors, namely:

(2) The higher the levels of state intervention in the economy, the greater the executive dominance in policy-making, and

  (2.1) The higher the levels of state intervention, the greater the ratio of managerial to nonmanagerial policies.

  (2.2) The greater the ratio of managerial decisions, the greater the relative dominance of the executive, but

(3) The extent to which the relationships in 2 hold and the magnitude of those relationships (that is, the magnitude of relative dominance) will be modified by the party system such that

    (3.1) The more seats in the legislature that are controlled by the administration party, the greater the magnitude of executive dominance.

The above hypotheses seem to be common for the investigations conducted in both Chile and Costa Rica. Are they given support by our findings? It seems obvious from previous discussions that both Chile and Costa Rica can readily be classified as having constitutional systems that have been observed as meaningful guides for political activity, in marked contrast to so many other Latin-American systems. Moreover, the constitutions of both countries; though differing in emphasis delegate an action-oriented role to the legislature. At the same time, we have noted aspects of both constitutions which seem to act as stumbling blocks to legislative dominance, such as the prohibition on immediate reelection in the Costa Rican case and the extraordinary legislative session in the case of Chile where the legislature can only submit bills that have the prior approval of the executive.

We can also see differences between the two countries in their respective applications of constitutional provisions. For example, while both systems utilize operative committee systems as integral parts of the policy process in the legislature, it is apparent that the resources available to the Chilean legislature to carry out this function far surpass the relatively meager staffing and research capabilities of the Costa Rican Legislative Assembly. The former does a significant amount of independent research while the latter was seen to be heavily dependent upon the information garnered by the executive.

These differences might be expected to manifest themselves most clearly in the modification stage of the policy process where legislative committees traditionally do much of their work. In fact, we saw this difference in the respective efforts of the Chilean and Costa Rican legislatures to modify executive policies. In the former, a great many executive bills are substantially changed while in the latter most executive proposals are changed insignificantly if at all.

Before attempting to attribute all variation, both within and between systems, to the constitutional framework, we should look at one of our primary factors that was hypothesized to affect relative dominance: state intervention in the economy. In both sets of data, though more systematically in the Chilean data, we found evidence that, in fact, the two states display a trend toward higher levels of activity in the economic sector. Looking at policy-making defined as law-making, we did not find support for the hypothesized relationship, at least in terms of relative dominance in the initiation stage. In fact, we found that, in both Chile and Costa Rica, the legislature rather than the executive was dominant, even as state intervention in the economy was on the upswing.

On the other hand, by broadening our concept of policy-making to include executive decrees, we constructed a total output measure of executive policies (decrees) compared with legislative policies (laws). On this dimension, state intervention in the economy was shown to be highly correlated with the relative dominance of the executive in Chile. Even though we also described Costa Rica as exhibiting executive dominance in this regard, the data failed to show any systematic correlation between increasing state intervention and that dominance. In part, this failure to substantiate the Beerian hypothesis in Costa Rica may be attributed to the lack of more discrete economic indicators.

As hypotheses 2.1 and 2.2 state, the state intervention variable may also operate indirectly on relative dominance through an intervening variable: managerial decisions. As we have noted in both Chile and Costa Rica, there was some difficulty in satisfactorily operationalizing the dimensions of that variable. One dimension was that of decisional specificity. Conceptualizing policy-making as law-making again, we found essentially no relationship between state intervention in the economy and increasing levels of specific decision-making. Nor did we find evidence in either country of executive dominance when decisions were specific in nature, especially in terms of policy initiation. In both countries, the legislature has maintained an active role in dealing with managerial policies (that is, specific policies).

The Chilean data, however, and to a lesser extent the Costa Rican data, do demonstrate executive dominance when executive decrees are considered in the policy context. By and large, executive decrees tend to fit closely the notion of policies as specific, hence managerial, in nature. Because we found that in both countries more decrees were issued than laws passed, the policy-making edge remains with the executive branch.

As discussed earlier in this essay, we would expect the role of the party system as it affects relative dominance to be manifested less in the initiation stage of the policy process than in the modification and acceptance-rejection stages. So while we might look closely initially at the level of state intervention in the economy as an explanatory factor, this may be modified in later policy stages by political party action. While both Chile and Costa Rica have multi-party systems, the latter system might more accurately be described as an essentially two-party system with minor parties acting more as interest groups within the legislature. That is, as discussed previously, there is the PLN party and the anti-PLN "party" with parties such as PASO and the newly formed PDC playing the pressure role.

While we found strong relationships between party support and/or opposition, party cohesion and relative dominance (that is, a decrease in the relative dominance of the executive) in Chile in all policy stages, in Costa Rica we found some clear indication that party opposition acted to decrease executive dominance only in the modification stage. It seems that there are at least two possible reasons for this difference in the two data sets. One reason involves the overall nature of the party systems. The existence of a vital, and stable, multi-party system with well-disciplined parties, such as characterizes Chile, tends to decrease the relative dominance of the executive in policy-making. On the other hand, while some observers have pointed to the disciplined nature of Costa Rican parties (Denton, 1971: 36), none of the parties, including the strong PLN, have maintained the mass-based support or organizational status of the bulk of their Chilean counterparts, both of which qualities appear to be dimensions of party vitality. Also, as discussed above, Costa Rica may be characterized as an essentially two-party system, with minor modifications.

The second reason for Chilean-Costa Rican differences on this dimension is methodological. Through the use of roll-call data, one of the authors was able to construct indexes of party cohesion in both the Chamber and Senate of the Chilean legislature. Roll-call voting is at a premium in Costa Rica, and so few roll calls were taken during the period under investigation that it would have been meaningless, and probably misleading, to have attempted to construct such indexes. Therefore, we have no direct evidence concerning how party members in the Legislative Assembly actually cast their ballots. In terms of the aggregate measure of percentage of seats in the legislature held by nonadministration parties, both sets of data show that this appeared to decrease the relative dominance of the executive.

One factor, that of public support, which was applied in the Chilean case, deserves brief attention at this point. As was made quite clear, systematic data do not exist in Chile to more adequately analyze the affects of this variable. Nevertheless, there is some evidence that does suggest the possible mediating effects of this factor upon the other hypothesized relationships. Unfortunately, the type of data, mainly survey-gathered, that would be necessary to examine this factor in Costa Rica is virtually non-existent. In Chile, the use of survey techniques in political inquiry is fairly well advanced and sophisticated. In Costa Rica, the population is far from being "Gallup-polled" to death. For example, not one of the several newspapers distributed in San José makes use of a Gallup-type opinion report.

SUGGESTIONS FOR FURTHER RESEARCH

This relatively modest effort at comparative legislative analysis by no means purports to provide answers for the numerous questions that political scientists in this area concern themselves with. Nevertheless, we strongly suggest that the framework of legislative-executive relations presented in this essay might be profitably used in further comparative studies. Also, we suggest that the hypotheses that were, in part, derived from the present research effort may be usefully employed in future efforts at accounting for relative dominance in the policy process.

As indicated in the introduction to this essay, many observers see a universal trend toward the relative dominance of the executive in policy-making, and we suggest that many of the same factors found to be operative in Chile and Costa Rica may be operative in other systems. Earlier in this essay, for example, we referred to the high levels of state intervention in the economy in France and Great Britain and noted that other authors have observed the strong relationship between this factor and executive dominance (Beer, 1966; Wahl, 1966). Moreover, these same writers referred to the party systems of both countries as having a modifying effect on relative dominance. By investigating these hypotheses within our policy stage framework, the precise operation of these variables might be more clearly specified.

The German case is somewhat unique and also suggests the need for further research in this area. First, it does not appear that the levels of state intervention are any higher than those in Chile although somewhat higher than those in Costa Rica. However, executive dominance in policy-making appears to far surpass that of the latter two countries. As Heidenheimer (1966: 133)) points out, the German Bundestag "has had great difficulty in developing proper techniques and styles through which to exercise control over the policies of the cabinet."

Second, the party factor appears as if it should increase legislative leverage, thereby decreasing executive dominance; yet it does not seem to have done so. For example, even given the fact that German governments often lack a parliamentary majority, the executive continues to dominate the policy process. Furthermore, the three principal parties all have cohesion scores over 90 percent which should also indicate a decrease in the relative dominance of the executive (Grosser, 1971: 454). These facts simply lead us to pose a question that we, at this time, are unable to answer: Why are the Chilean and Costa Rican legislatures so much more influential than those of such countries as Germany and Great Britain which supposedly exist in a more "advanced" and "democratic" milieu?

To answer this question, it may well be necessary to expand our list of hypotheses concerning relative dominance. One possible direction to move, at least in the German case, has been suggested by students of German politics. It appears that the parties, particularly the CDU/CSU and SPD, are highly compromise oriented (Loewenberg, 1961: 95). Thus, the parties will work out agreements on proposals instead of engaging in legislative conflict as in Chile and Costa Rica. In order for the parties to decrease executive dominance, it may not be enough for the opposition to control the legislature and to be (individually) highly cohesive. Rather, it may also be necessary for the opposition parties to be non-compromisors. Certainly, the German case suggests the need to test this proposition cross-nationally.

Another area of research needed is a closer examination of legislative committee systems on a cross-national basis. What, for example, leads some countries, such as Chile, Costa Rica, and the United States, to have relatively strong committees while others, such as Great Britain, have weak ones? Even though we pointed out the obstacles faced by Costa Rican committees (for example, lack of adequate staffing), it appears that the system is still more effective than that of Great Britain where all government legislation "goes through [Parliament] without substantial amendment" (Crick, 1970: 51-52). Here again, one might profitably apply our framework, possibly with some extensions and modifications, to begin to answer these and other questions of importance to students of legislative politics.

Notes

1. In fairness, it should be pointed out that the editors generally recognize the shortcomings of their volumes. Agor (1971a: xxvii), for example, notes the exploratory nature of all the contributions to his volume. An additional problem is the country-by-country approach of the contributions. This approach, of course, makes adequately generalizing from case studies impossible.

2. In addition to the volume edited by Agor, which includes his article on the decisional role of the Chilean Senate previously published in the book edited by Kornberg and Musolf (1970), one should see his book-length study (1971b).

3. At least this is what most of the research on United States legislatures would lead us to believe (inter alia, Fenno, 1966: Jewell and Patterson, 1966).

4. Unfortunately, as is discussed in the next section, this measure could not be applied to Chile because of the nature of reporting defeated bills. The Chilean study relies, therefore, more on interviews and case studies.

5. This measure is suggested in a study by Beer (1966).

6. Note, for instance, the conflict in Chile over the executive's decree-making powers. Two fascinating and insightful studies on this and related topics are offered by Richards Piedrabuena G. (1970) and Arturo Olavarría Bravo (1966-1970). Similar executive-legislative conflicts were reported to one of the authors in Costa Rica by legislators and former legislators.

7. The regulations concerning the convocation of ordinary and extraordinary legislatures are contained in the Constitution, Articles 56 and 57. Extraordinary legislatures may also be convened by the President of the Senate upon written request by the majority of Senators or Deputies. In such sessions, anyone may originate a bill without presidential sponsorship.

8. *Leyes de gracia* are essentially bills granting small to moderate pensions to individual persons.

9. In Chile, a bill passes through two basic floor discussions, one in which legislators vote whether or not to consider the project at all and a second in which they consider proposed amendments. The first is the "discussion in general"; the second, the "discussion in particular."

10. Tapia (1960: 48) has found a very similar situation for the period 1938-1958.

11. The combined index for state intervention was derived by adding the figures for each indicator and dividing by three.

12. We defined Alessandri's support in terms of electoral support and roll call votes. The latter was necessary in order to ascertain what percentage of Radicals (about 10) continuously supported him.

13. Bills can be introduced into the Legislative Assembly by private citizens yet they require the counter-signature of a *diputado*. In a real sense, they can be considered as essentially legislative bills.

14. Unless otherwise noted, all tables and graphs presented here were derived from data collected by one of the authors.

15. These experts were a diverse group of ten deputies and former deputies of the Legislative Assembly. Their selection as interviewees was made based on the following criteria:

(1) *Length of Service.* Only those who had served more than one term were chosen.

(2) *Position held in the legislature.* Two of those selected were former presidents of the Legislative Assembly and several occupied important posts in their respective party caucuses.

(3) *Experience outside of the legislature.* Several of the interviewees have held (and presently hold) administrative positions during one or more of the presidential administrations in our study.

(4) *Party membership.* All major parties were represented. Excluded were representatives of the newly organized, and still minor, Christian Democratic Party and Socialist Action Party.

16. The sample size is only 177 in this table because the remainder of the bills were, by vote of the whole legislature, *dispensados con los trámites,* or sent directly to the first floor debate without being processed by committees. This procedure of dispensing with the committee phase is very common, accounting for almost half of our sample. It generally occurs when no significant opposition is foreseen by the leadership and/or when the legislation is relatively minor.

18. Conceptual definitions of the degree of modification are the following: (1) no change—verbatim acceptance of original policy proposals, slight change—

mostly rearranging words rather than substance; (2) moderate change—rearranging and modifying both words and substance, but with the general intent of bill unchanged; (3) significant change—much substantive modification which would affect some of the bill's original intent; (4) complete change—original intent of bill modification completely with no resemblance to original proposal.

19. Recall our caveat concerning the oversampling of defeated bills in our sample. This would cause these ratios to be inflated. Nevertheless, their relationship to each other would remain unchanged; that is, about three times as many legislative-sponsored bills as executive sponsored proposals are rejected.

20. For a discussion of the formal regulations concerning the passage of bills through the legislature, see Asamblea Legislativa (1970).

21. Although this generalization is not based on a systematic analysis of the data, the phenomenon occurred with some regularity throughout the time period under investigation. The use of the veto, however, is quite seldom invoked; only three bills in our sample were vetoed.

22. Interview in August, 1970, with Fernando Lara Bustamante, former Unión Nacional (PUN) deputy and cabinet minister during the Trejos administration.

23. From an interview with Fernando Volio Jiménez, former Ambassador to the United Nation, former President of the Legislative Assembly and currently Vice-Minister of Education, August 5, 1970.

24. One of many problems of data collection in Latin America manifested itself here. The documents from which these data were taken wre often difficult to obtain, either in the country or, being somewhat overly optimistic, from the Library of Congress in the United States. A useful source was the Lati-American Studies section of the University of Florida library, yet even that institution held incomplete records.

References

AGOR, W. [ed.] (1971a) Latin American Legislatures: Their Role and Influence. New York: Praeger Special Studies.
――― (1971b) The Chilean Senate. Austin: University of Texas Press.
――― (1969) "The Chilean senate—internal distribution of influence." Ph.D. dissertation. Madison: University of Wisconsin.
ANDERSON, L., M. W. WATTS and A. R. WILCOX (1966) Legislative Roll-Call Analysis. Evanston: Northwestern University Press.
Asamblea Legislativa (1970) Reglamento de orden, dirección y disciplina interior. San José: Imprenta Nacional.
BAKER, C. (1971) "The Costa Rican Legislative Assembly: a preliminary evaluation of the decisional function," pp. 53-111 in W. Agor (ed.) Latin American Legislatures: Their Role and Influence. New York: Praeger Special Studies.
BAUER, R. and K. GERGEN [eds.] (1968) The Study of Policy Formation. New York: Free Press.
BEER, S. (1966) "The British legislature and the problem of mobilizing consent," pp. 30-48 in E. Frank (ed.) Lawmakers in a Changing World. Englewood Cliffs, N.J.: Prentice-Hall.
BIBBY, J. (1966) "Committee characteristics and legislative oversight of administration." Midwest Journal of Political Science 10 (February): 78-98.

BLONDEL, J. (1969-70) "Legislative behavior: some steps toward cross-national measurement." Government and Opposition 5 (Winter): 67-85.
BULNES, R. C. (1967) Relaciones y conflictos entre los órganos del poder estatal. Santiago: Editorial Jurídica.
BUSEY, J. L. (1964) "Costa Rica: a meaningful democracy," in M. Needler (ed.) Political Systems of Latin America. New Jersey: Van Nostrand.
――― (1962) Notes on Costa Rican democracy. Boulder: University of Colorado.
CRICK, B. (1970) "Parliament in the British political system," in A. Kornberg and L. Musolf (eds.) Legislatures in Developmental Perspective. Durham, N.C.: Duke University Press.
CUMPLIDO, F. (1970) "Constitución política de 1925: hoy, crisis de las instituciones políticos chilenos." Cuadernos de la realidad nacional 5 (September): 25-40.
DENTON, C. F. (1971) Patterns of Costa Rican Politics. Boston: Allyn and Bacon.
Diario de Sesiones de la Cámara (1958-70). Santiago.
Diario de Sesiones del Senado (1958-70). Santiago.
Diario oficial de la República de Chile (1958-70). Santiago.
EDELMANN, A. (1969) Latin American Government and Politics. Homewood: Dorsey Press.
FENNO, R. F., Jr., (1966) The Power of the Purse: Appropriations Politics in Congress. Boston: Little, Brown.
FREEMAN, J. L. (1966) The Political Process: Executive Bureau-Legislative Committee Relations. New York: Random House.
FRIEDRICH, C. (1950) Constitutional Government and Democracy. Boston: Ginn and Company.
GIL. F. (1966) The Political System of Chile. Boston: Houghton-Mifflin.
GÓMEZ, R. (1961) "Latin American executives: essence and variation." Journal of Inter-American Studies 3 (January): 81-96.
GRIFFITH, E. S. (1967) Congress: Its Contemporary Role. New York: New York University Press.
GROSSER, A. (1971) "The evolution of European parliaments," pp. 445-458 in M. Dogan and R. Rose (eds.) European Politics: A Reader. Boston: Little, Brown.
GUZMAN D., J. [ed.] (1964) Nueva sociedad, vieja constitución. Santiago: Editorial Orbe.
HEIDENHEIMER, A. J. (1966) The Governments of Germany. New York: Thomas Y. Growell.
HUGHES, S. W. (1971) "Governmental decision-making in Chile." Ph.D. dissertation. Chapel Hill: University of North Carolina.
HUITT, R. K. (1966) "Congress, the durable partner," pp. 9-29 in E. Frank (ed.) Lawmakers in a Changing World. Englewood Cliffs, N.J.: Prentice-Hall.
JEWELL, M. E. and S. C. PATTERSON (1966) The Legislative Process in the United States. New York: Random House.
KORNBERG, A. [ed.] (1973) Legislatures in Comparative Perspective. New York: David McKay.
――― and L. D. MUSOLF [eds.] (1970) Legislatures in Developmental Perspective. Durham, N.C.: Duke University Press.
LAMBERT, J. (1967) Latin America: Social Structures and Political Institutions. Berkeley, Ca.: University of California Press.
LINDBERG, L. (1966) "The role of the European parliament in an emerging European community," pp. 101-128 in E. Frank (ed.) Lawmakers in a Changing World. Englewood Cliffs, N.J.: Prentice-Hall.

LOEWENBERG, G. (1972) "Comparative legislative research," pp. 3-21 in S. Patterson and J. Wahlke (eds.) Comparative Legislative Behavior: Frontiers of Research. New York: John Wiley.
——— (1961) "Parliamentarism in Western Germany: the functioning of the Bundestag." American Political Science Review 60 (March).
MIJESKI, K. J. (1971) "The executive-legislative policy process in Costa Rica." Ph.D. dissertation. Chapel Hill: University of North Carolina.
MONGE A., C. (1959) Historia de Costa Rica. San José: Imprenta Trejos.
OLAVARRÍA B., A. (1966-1970) Chile bajo la democracia cristiana. Santiago: Editorial Nascimento.
PATTERSON, S. and J. WAHLKE [eds.] (1972) Comparative Legislative Behavior: Frontiers of Research. New York: John Wiley.
PIEDRABUENA G., R. (1970) La reforma constitucional. Santiago: Ediciones Encina.
POLSBY, N. W. (1963) Community Power and Political Theory. New Haven: Yale University Press.
RANNEY, A. [ed.] (1968) Political Science and Public Policy. Chicago: Markham.
RECABARREN, R. (1969) La toma de razón de los decretos y resoluciones. Santiago: Editorial Jurídica.
ROBINSON, J. (1962) Congress and Foreign Policy Making. Homewood: Dorsey.
SCHER, S. (1963) "Conditions for legislative control." Journal of Politics 25 (August): 526-551.
SCHULZ, A. (1972) "The role of legislatures and comparative research." Journal of Comparative Administration 4 (May): 117-124.
SCOTT, R. (1958) "Legislatures and legislation," pp. 290-332 in H. Davies (ed.) Government and Politics in Latin America. New York: The Ronald Press.
SHARKANSKY, I. (1965) "An appropriations subcommittee and its client agencies: a comparative study of supervision and control." American Political Science Review 59 (September): 622-628.
SILVERT, K. (1961) The Conflict Society: Reaction and Revolution in Latin America. New York: Harper and Row.
SINDING, S. W. (1970) "Political participation, government expenditures and economic growth in Chile." Ph.D. dissertation. Chapel Hill: University of North Carolina.
TAPIA V., J. (1960) La técnica legislativa. Santiago: Editorial Jurídica.
TOMASEK, R. D. (1968) "Costa Rica," in B. G. Burnett and K. Johnson (eds.) Political Forces in Latin America: Dimensions of the Quest for Stability. Belmont, Ca.: Wadsworth.
WAHL, N. (1966) "The Fifth Republic: from last word to afterthought," pp. 49-64 in E. Frank (ed.) Lawmakers in a Changing World. Englewood Cliffs, N.J.: Prentice-Hall.

STEVEN W. HUGHES is Assistant Professor of Political Science at California State College, Stanislaus. Born in Los Angeles, California, in 1944, he received his B.A. from Whittier College and his Ph.D. from the University of North Carolina, Chapel Hill, in 1971. His research on the Chilean government was carried out in 1970 in Chile.

KENNETH J. MIJESKI is Assistant Professor of Political Science at East Tennessee State University. A native of Miami, Florida, he received his B.A. (International Affairs) from Florida State University in 1966. His graduate work was done at the University of North Carolina, Chapel Hill, where he received his Ph.D. in 1971. Research he did for his doctoral thesis in Costa Rica in 1970 forms the basis for the discussion of that country in this paper.